Hidden From History

Women who changed the world

Peter Frost

manifesto

First published 2016 by Manifesto Press

© Peter Frost

978-1-907464-04-1

Typeset in Garamond and Gill
Printed in Britain by Russell Press

Front cover illustration by Jon Schwochert

CONTENTS

PREFACE

'LL never forget the way Peter Frost — "Frosty" to Morning Star staff and readers alike — became a regular columnist at the people's paper four years ago.

A chance article on the 80th anniversary of the great Kinder Scout trespass of 1932 made me and Ben Chacko — then my deputy on the features desk, now the paper's editor — immediate converts. Here was a writer who could bring the past alive: tell important political stories but make them so fresh and engaging you felt you were chatting to a friend in the pub rather than reading about a historical event.

We wanted more, and we got it — within days of our commissioning a weekly column from Frosty we had articles streaming in on every topic under the sun, from how canal privatisation threatened the water vole to the impact of Charlie Chaplin on film.

The right sometimes accuse the left of being joyless or unpatriotic. Anyone suffering from this delusion should read Frosty's Ramblings in the Star every Friday, every article shot through with humour and a love of the flora, fauna and wonderful people who have made this country.

So many of these people, the ones who have really made a difference, are ignored by Establishment histories and narratives which focus on prime ministers and presidents, aristocrats and generals; and, overwhelmingly, on men, men, men.

So it's wonderful now to see this book published — celebrating and commemorating the lives of close to 40 remarkable women, women who in many cases changed the world but who are all too often ignored.

Each entry originated as an article in the Morning Star and each bears the unmistakeable style of Peter Frost — the chatty and cheerful voice of a true raconteur.

Anyone who thinks women deserve more attention and credit from our historians should read this book. I enjoyed every piece, and look forward to reading many more of Frosty's columns in the future.

ROS SITWELL
Assistant editor, Morning Star

For Ann

INTRODUCTION

Back in 2012 I was writing articles on the 80th anniversary of the momentous Kinder Trespass for most of the outdoor magazines in Britain. I had recently retired from a 25-year job writing and broadcasting about leisure in the British countryside.

My half a century of journalism had started as editor of the Young Communist League magazine Challenge. A period in television news with the international news agency Visnews followed.

After that I moved to Soviet news agency Novosti and then to the editor's chair of the biggest camping and caravanning magazine in the world. I finished as director of communications for the 100-year-old and half-a-million-strong Camping and Caravanning Club.

It was a wonderful job, my wife Ann and I toured Britain and the world. We camped, caravanned or motor-caravanned in 42 countries. My company car was a Volkswagen camper.

One highlight of the job came when I was able to assist Nelson Mandela's Rainbow Nation in the democratising of its fast-growing tourist industry. I helped establish the first campsite quality control and grading system in the whole of Africa. The system and the site-guides based on it are still in use. On a South African campsite you can look out from your tent and see elephants, zebras, springboks, wildebeest, ostriches and even lions come to drink at the floodlit waterhole. No wonder camping is growing ever more popular in the country.

I also advised the Croatian Tourist Board on sustainable tourism after the Yugoslav wars. One in five visitors was a nudist, only the naturists had holidayed in Croatia in the dark days of the war and they wanted to encourage tourists in clothes too.

In Britain, in my Kinder Trespass articles I was trying to inject a bit of political context into this event which led to the establishment of our wonderful National Park movement as well as legislation allowing public access to our countryside. I had been appointed by the Labour government as a trustee of one of our National Parks, and now I was seeing how David Cameron and Nick Clegg were slashing funding and support for these jewels of our green and pleasant land.

Also after two years of Cameron's coalition I was angry, frustrated and desperate to do something to raise my voice about these posh Eton boys who thought they had a God-given right to rule the country on behalf of their millionaire friends. By now I was a member of the Labour Party and indeed chaired my CLP for a period — but that wasn't enough I wanted somewhere else I could make my voice heard more widely.

I asked the features department at the Morning Star if they would like something on the politics of the Kinder Trespass. As so often, the real history of the Trespass, the fact that it was conceived and mostly organised by young communist Benny Rothman and his YCL comrades, had been forgotten, or more likely politically censored. I knew that this was a story that needed to be told. The Star said yes, and when I sent the first article they immediately asked for another on the same subject.

They then asked if I could do a more regular column on the environment and countryside issues. When I agreed my wife Ann and the then features editor Ros Sitwell (now assistant editor) came up with what I thought a most disrespectful general title — Frosty's Ramblings. I was overruled on the title, but my Ramblings still appear in the Star most Fridays.

Later I would expand my Star writings mostly in the field of lesser-known aspects of political history. I had always been annoyed by the fact that many good people have been written out of history. These include women, left-wing heroes, many of them communists, and of course, homosexuals.

Perhaps the worst recent example of this was the recent, and otherwise excellent and inspiring film, Pride. How could it be that the fact that one of the main characters Mark Ashton was general secretary of the Young Communist League is not even mentioned? The film almost avoids the 'C' word altogether, it is said because if it mentioned communists it wouldn't be distributed in the US.

I love to discover and introduce readers to some of the forgotten corners of working-class history and how important left-wing people and ideas were at the time. The same applies to women, so many have been hidden from history. Hopefully this book goes a small way to putting that right.

Please remember this book is an anthology of existing writings already published in the People's Paper. If you think I have left your own particular champion out it probably isn't by choice. The book certainly isn't my list of top female heroes either. If it was it would certainly include, among many others, the following: Anne Frank, the Jewish girl who hid from the nazis and left an inspirational diary; Emma Goldman, who played a pivotal role in the development of anarchist political philosophy in both North America and Europe; Rosa Luxemburg, German communist leader who was shot and her body thrown in a in Berlin canal by extreme right-wing forces.

Angela Davis, Communist Party USA leader in the 1960s. Rose Schneiderman, US union leader, socialist, and feminist who coined my favourite political slogan, Bread and Roses; Jayaben Desai, leader of the mainly female Asian strikers in the epic Grunwick dispute in London in 1976...

Labour MP Ellen Wilkinson, one of Britain's first female MPs, founding member of the British Communist Party who marched to London with the Jarrow marchers; Rosalind Franklin, the unsung hero of DNA, Franklin's X-ray images of the double helix provided the data that Francis Crick and James Watson used to win their Nobel Prize; Mary Jane Seacole, a mixed-race, Jamaican-born nurse made her own way to the Crimean front line, where she tended to wounded British soldiers; Doreen Lawrence, the mother of murdered black British teenager Stephen Lawrence and now a leading campaigner against racism and injustice.

So far I haven't written at length about any of these outstanding women for the Morning Star. I do intend to when a suitable occasion arises so keep reading the paper — the best may still be yet to come.

However many of my favourite female heroes are featured. This year we mark the centenary of the declaration of the Irish Republic at

Easter 1916. Many women played their part in these epic events not least Countess Constance Markievicz.

Music hall quenn Marie Lloyd is here too, she played a massive part in bringing unions to the stage. Show business and the movies both have their share of women, far more than just pretty faces and beautiful bodies. Many of them played their part in the struggle for justice and progress.

Among the women in this book not all are heroes. Ruth Ellis is perhaps the ultimate victim, the last woman hanged in Britain. Today we hope, she would have received more sympathetic treatment as a lifelong victim of abuse. Belle Elmore on the other hand was a second-rate music hall performer and a strikebreaker to boot. But she still didn't deserve to die at the hands of her husband Dr Crippen!

Suffragettes and civil rights fighters are here in force of course, along with canal boaters, members of the Women's Institute and the Land Army, writers, flyers, early socialists, and a score or two of diverse women who, to quote Mao Zedong, "Hold up half the sky." .

Books like this are never individual efforts. I need to thank my wife Ann, my granddaughter Lizzie already at just 16 the youngest-ever paid employee of the Labour Party. Lizzie worked recruiting young voters as part of the missing million project in the 2015 general election. Her knowledge of environmental issues too has often helped with my writing. It is good to know a new generation of progressive women is ready to take up the fight.

Lizzie's mother Jane is often a source of good ideas for articles. Thanks too must go to Ros Sitwell, Ben Chacko, Faye Lipson, Kadeem Simmonds, Michal Boncza and many other Morning Star staff past and present and to many other comrades and friends far too numerous to mention.

The opinions and mistakes however are all mine.

Peter Frost

February 2016

WHEN MRS BARBOUR'S ARMY WON THE DAY

MARY BARBOUR

Published December 18 2015 the Centenary of the Glasgow Rent Strike.

One of the largest demonstrations ever seen in Glasgow took place 100 years ago towards the end of 1915.

Willie Gallacher, who would later become a Communist MP, caught the mood beautifully. He called the huge protest of thousands of rent-striking housewives accompanied by shipyard and engineering workers "Mrs Barbour's Army."

So who was this Mrs Barbour whose army had converged on the sheriff's courts in the centre of Glasgow a century ago this week?

Mary Barbour was born on February 22 1875 in Kilbarchan in Renfrewshire, the third of seven children born to carpet-weaver James Rough and his wife Jane Gavin. When the family moved to Elderslie in 1887, Mary herself began work in the carpet mills.

In 1896 she married David Barbour and they settled in Govan beside the Clyde near Glasgow. Mary joined the Kinning Park Co-operative Guild — at the time the first co-operative guild in Scotland — and it was here her political education started.

She joined the Independent Labour Party and became active in the socialist Sunday school movement.

In early 1914, despite the "all in this together" attitude of WWI, landlords increased rents steeply. Landlords it seems haven't changed much in a 100 years.

Women's Labour League president Mary Laird formed the Glasgow Women's Housing Association and in Govan in June 1915 the first signs of really militant resistance arose, led by Mary Barbour. She formed the South Govan Women's Housing Association.

As a working-class and working woman with two sons and a husband in the shipyards, she was deeply involved in local working-class struggle.

This was at a time when Clydebank was seen as a hotbed of socialist ideas and protest — Glaswegians were not afraid to protest against the jingoism of WWI.

In June 1916 another rent strike leader, Helen Crawfurd, launched the Women's Peace Crusade to oppose the war.

Many of the leading figures of what was called Red Clydeside were women — as well as Mary Barbour there were Agnes Dollen, Crawfurd and Jessie Stephens. Male leaders included John Maclean, Willie Gallacher and David Kirkwood. Mary Barbour's Army was actively involved in organising tenant committees and local resistance to sheriff seizures and forced evictions.

The rent strike quickly spread all over Glasgow, where 25,000 households refused to pay rent and hundreds of people turned out to stop evictions. In panic, David Lloyd George's government quickly passed the Rent Restrictions Act of 1915. This Act helped improve the legal position of working-class tenants throughout Britain in their dealings with private landlords.

Barbour's contribution to the strikes encouraged her involvement in Red Clydeside Glasgow politics — and what politics!

On January 31 1919 a massive rally was held in George Square, in the heart of Glasgow — 90,000 women and men filled the square to support the campaign for a 40-hour week and better conditions for workers.

The red flag was raised in the crowd, the police read the Riot Act and tanks and soldiers were brought in as the government feared the protests would turn to a Bolshevik revolution. The leaders of the strike were arrested and charged with "instigating and inciting large crowds of persons to form part of a riotous mob." Gallacher was sentenced to five months in jail.

In 1920 Barbour stood for Labour and won in the municipal elections for Fairfield ward in Govan. Sadly she was not a candidate in the 1922 general election when a number of male Red Clydesiders, including David Kirkwood, James Maxton, John Wheatley and Manny Shinwell were elected to the House of Commons.

Willie Gallacher would be elected as Communist MP for East Fife, but not until 1935.

Barbour went on to build a huge reputation as one of Labour's first female councillors in Glasgow. She campaigned for the introduction of municipal banks, wash-houses, laundries and baths, free milk for schoolchildren, child welfare centres and play areas, home help and pensions for mothers.

From 1924 until 1927 she served as the first woman bailie — the Scottish equivalent of an alderman — on Glasgow Corporation and was appointed one of Glasgow's first female magistrates.

Barbour pioneered the city's first family planning centre — the Women's Welfare and Advisory Clinic — in 1925 and also chaired its first committee, raising sufficient funds to employ female doctors and nurses. She continued as a councillor until 1931. After retiring from council work she still continued her activities on a range of housing, welfare and co-operative committees. She organised seaside outings for the children of poor families in Glasgow.

Mary Barbour died on April 2 1958 aged 83. She is not forgotten and the spirit of her wonderful army still marches through Glasgow's streets beside the Clyde.

AN EARLY ENVIRONMENTAL CHAMPION

RACHEL CARSON

Published Thursday September 27 2012 on the 50th anniversary of the publication of Rachel Carson's groundbreaking book Silent Spring .

We all owe a tremendous debt to Rachel Carson who published her book Silent Spring on September 27 1962 — exactly half a century ago. Almost single-handedly the book launched the environmental and green movements first in the US and then all across the globe.

Carson was already a well-known writer on natural history but her new book was different. Silent Spring inspired widespread public concerns with pesticides and damage they were inflicting on the environment.

In 10 years Silent Spring, with its warnings of a spring without birdsong, would shift public opinion enough to facilitate the ban of the widely used and very profitable agricultural pesticide DDT in the US.

The book explained the detrimental effects of pesticides on the environment, particularly as they moved up the food chain. Many birds were affected. Even the most iconic US bird the bald eagle was close to extinction due to heavy and sustained pesticide use.

Carson went further; she accused the agricultural chemical industry of spreading lies and the authorities of accepting industry claims uncritically. Predictably the greedy chemical industry including companies like Monsanto — so involved in today's GM battles — fought back.

Tame scientists were wheeled out to accuse Carson of being a "hysterical woman." Her book was described as panicky non-scientific nonsense. Despite the attacks the book has never been out of print in

50 years and it was recently named one of the 25 greatest science books of all time by the editors of the prestigious US Discover magazine. It is considered a foundation stone of the world conservation movement.

Silent Spring was inspired by a letter written in 1958 by Carson's friend Olga Owens Huckins to the Boston Herald, describing the death of numerous birds around her property resulting from the aerial spraying of DDT.

That letter prompted Carson to turn her attention to environmental problems caused by the uncontrolled use of chemical pesticides. She herself had been concerned about the wider effect of DDT and other pesticides that had been part of the Pacific war effort since 1940. The book argued that massive pesticide use was harming and even killing not only animals and birds but also humans.

The book makes it clear that Carson was not seeking the banning or complete withdrawal of useful pesticides but was instead encouraging responsible and carefully managed use, with careful study of how the chemicals affected each ecosystem.

The book and the uproar it caused saw President John F Kennedy direct his science advisory committee to investigate Carson's claims. It agreed with her warnings and the result was stronger controls on chemical pesticides.

In fact DDT was banned for agricultural use in the US in 1972. But only in the US, just two years later Cecily Watkins-Pitchford, the wife of one of Britain's best wildlife writers died in her Northampton-shire garden after suffering from chemical spraying by a neighbouring farmer. DDT wasn't banned in Britain until 1984.

No responsible person believes that insect-borne disease should be ignored. Rachel Carson asked if it is either wise or responsible to attack the problem by methods that actually make it worse.

DDT isn't your average pesticide. It's the only one with a Nobel Prize. Paul Mueller won it in 1948 for having discovered its insecticidal properties. Joni Mitchell sang: "Hey, farmer, farmer put away your DDT now" surely the only pop song about a pesticide.

DDT still has its uses today. Many African governments — South Africa included — are advocating the use of DDT believing that it's their best hope against malaria, a disease that kills at least three million people each year — a large proportion of them children. Hundreds of millions also suffer from the disease but survive.

Malaria is spread by a parasite transmitted by mosquitoes. There are two major ways to combat the disease — killing the parasite or killing the mosquito. Killing the parasite is difficult. Many older drugs are no longer effective, new ones expensive. Destroying the mosquito has long been the preferred way to fight malaria.

DDT does a good job killing mosquitoes at first and it is cheap compared with other insecticides. But mosquitoes get immune to it quickly. Despite that, used sensibly DDT still has a place in our armoury of weapons to be used against killer insect-borne diseases. The UN Environment Programme however says that DDT can cause major environmental harm. It wants to add it to a "dirty dozen" for worldwide reduction or eventual elimination.

The DDT debate goes on, but it's a wiser more educated debate because Rachel Carson wrote her Silent Spring 50 years ago.

Without her all the decisions would still be made behind closed doors by the profit-driven agricultural chemical transnationals. I don't think they would mind a silent spring as long as they could still hear the cash registers ringing.

COMRADE MARILYN

MARILYN MONROE

Published Tuesday January 8 2012 as the FBI released previously secret files on the film star's political life.

"Are you or have you ever been a member of the Communist Party?" Recent FBI papers still haven't answered that question about Marilyn Monroe. Almost exactly 60 years ago arch-sexist Hugh Hefner launched Playboy magazine. When it came to choosing the cover girl and first centre-spread there was no contest. It just had to be Marilyn Monroe. Who else appeared to match the American male dream of a shapely sex bomb who was both pliant, subservient and available?

A dizzy, bubbly blonde with no ideas or opinions of her own — for so many, that was the image they had of Monroe. Many still have that image today. Just imagine how middle America might have reacted on discovering that its favourite sex icon was a communist.

Throughout her life and even more after her death, the tabloid media had a field day with Monroe's private life. If you believe the catalogue of scurrilous stories, she had slept with President Jack Kennedy, his brother Bobby and scores of film stars, male and female, from Marlon Brando to Elizabeth Taylor.

The lists were both comprehensive and imaginative. Albert Einstein and the plumber who came to fix her toilet were both allegedly welcomed into her bed. The stories, true or not, certainly fed millions of male fantasies. But Monroe's image and the reality were as different as chalk and cheese. The supposedly dizzy brainless blonde actually had great intelligence and a real social conscience.

She never tried to hide her left-wing political opinions. She was pro-union and anti-racist. She campaigned against nuclear weapons and for civil rights. In segregated America she fought to get black performers onto previously white-only stages. She got Ella Fitzgerald her first booking in a Los Angles club that had previously only booked white artists. "Book Ella and I'll sit in the front row for every performance," she told the club owner — who wasn't slow to realise that Monroe's presence would bring in the crowds.

At the height of the anti-communist witch-hunts she worked with and eventually married communist playwright Arthur Miller. "Miller wouldn't have married me if I was just a dumb blonde," she told the press.

She employed communists and communist sympathisers at home and in her film production company. Her doctors and therapists were close to the Communist Party or indeed actual members. Whether these people actually held — or told people they held — Communist Party membership cards is of little consequence.

In the US of Joe McCarthy's witch-hunts, the House Un-American Activities Committee hearings and the Hollywood blacklists it wasn't the kind of information people bandied about.

After much campaigning and many Freedom of Information requests FBI files on Marilyn Monroe that could not be located earlier this year have finally been unearthed and published. They contain gems like this, from an anonymous male caller, who phoned the Daily News to report that the actress's company, Marilyn Monroe Productions, was filled with communists and that money from the company was being used to finance communist activities. The caller said Miller's marriage to Monroe during a Jewish ceremony less than a month earlier was a cover-up. Miller, the man said, "was still a member of the Communist Party and was their cultural front man."

The files are not just vague and anonymous — they are far from complete and have been heavily censored. Other FBI files have not yet been released and the Bureau is still resisting anybody looking at them.

When Monroe's house was remodelled after her death an extensive network of bugging devices was discovered.

The newly released files do show how frightened the FBI was that Monroe would be revealed as a communist sympathiser. In fact the film star had never been ashamed of her opinions or her communist-leaning friends.

The records reveal her association with Frederick Vanderbilt Field, who was disinherited from his wealthy family over his leftist views. Field was universally described by the US media as a "millionaire communist."

Monroe made no secret of her friendship with the Fields. She took a trip to Mexico where they were living in self-imposed exile with a group of other communists. Field's autobiography devotes an entire chapter to Monroe's Mexico trip. He tells readers: "She talked mostly about herself and some of the people who had been or still were important to her.

"She told us about her strong feelings for civil rights, for black equality, as well as her admiration for what was being done in China, her anger at red-baiting and McCarthyism and her hatred of [FBI top dog] J Edgar Hoover."

Monroe's FBI file begins in 1955 and mostly focuses on her travels and associations, searching for signs of leftist views and possible ties to communism. One entry, which previously had been almost completely censored, tells us that Monroe and other entertainers sought visas to visit Soviet Russia — a terrible crime in the eyes of Hoover's FBI.

For all the focus on Monroe's closeness to suspected communists, the bureau never found any proof she was an actual member of the party. "Subject's views are very positively and concisely leftist; however, if she is being actively used by the Communist Party, it is not general knowledge among those working with the movement in Los Angeles," an entry in Monroe's file states. If they had simply asked Monroe could have told them that.

Just before her mysterious death in 1962 she gave a quote to a journalist. "Please don't make me a joke. End the interview with what I believe," she told him. Fifty years after her death, and with her still making headlines, that is surely the least we can do for Marilyn Monroe.

We'll give her the last word because what she believed in speaks for itself. "What I really want to say is that what the world needs is a feeling of kinship. Everybody — stars, labourers, blacks, Jews, Arabs — we're all brothers!"

SHE SAT DOWN FOR FREEDOM

ROSA PARKS

Published February 13 2013 on the centenary of Rosa's birth.

The story of Rosa Parks, one of the most important figures in the battle against racism, who was born 100 years ago this month It was a simple act. In 1955 department store seamstress Rosa Parks, on her way home from a long day at work refused to give up her seat in the "coloured section" to a standing white passenger. It was an act that would light a flame that would burn from Montgomery, Alabama, all across the United States and then across the globe.

Parks' simple act would change the world and open the way, not least, to a black president in the White House. If you don't believe me ask Barack Obama. He will tell you the debt he and all black people owe to Rosa Parks. He has been leading the celebrations and the tributes to her all this month — 100 years after her birth.

So who was this remarkable woman and how did she come to change the world we all live in? Parks was born Rosa Louise McCauley in Tuskegee, Alabama, on February 4 1913 to Leona, a teacher, and James McCauley, a carpenter.

When her parents separated she moved with her mother to Pine Level, just outside the state capital of Montgomery. There she grew up on a farm with her grandparents, mother and younger brother Sylvester.

In the southern states black people lived under racist Jim Crow laws, segregation was imposed in public facilities and retail stores, including public transport. Electoral laws effectively disfranchised black voters.

Parks recalled her school days in Pine Level. School buses took white students to their new school and black students had to walk to theirs. When the Ku Klux Klan marched down the street in front of their house, Parks recalls her grandfather guarding the front door with a shotgun. Her Montgomery Industrial School, founded and staffed by white northerners for black children, was burned down twice.

In 1932 Rosa married Raymond Parks, a barber from Montgomery. Raymond was a member of the National Association for the Advancement of Coloured People (NAACP), which at the time was collecting money to support the defence of the "Scottsboro Boys," a group of black men falsely accused of raping two white women.

At her husband's urging, Parks finished her high school studies. Despite the Jim Crow laws she succeeded in registering to vote on her third try. Parks became active in the civil rights movement, joined the Montgomery chapter of the NAACP, and was elected secretary. She continued as secretary until 1957.

Although never a member of the Communist Party, she and her husband did attend communist meetings. Some were about the Scottsboro case in which several black men had been falsely accused of rape. It was a campaign that had been brought to prominence by the CPUSA.

Parks worked as a housekeeper and seamstress for Clifford and Virginia Durr, a white couple. Politically liberal, the Durrs became her friends. They encouraged — and eventually helped sponsor — Parks in the summer of 1955 to attend the Highlander Folk School, a left-wing education centre for activism in workers' rights and racial equality in Tennessee.

Close to the Communist Party, the Highlander Folk's School was the place where the old slave ballad We Shall Overcome was turned into the anthem of the civil rights movement and so many other campaigns.

In August 1955, black teenager Emmett Till was beaten and shot after reportedly flirting with a young white woman while visiting relatives in Mississippi. In November 1955 Parks attended a mass meeting in Montgomery that addressed this notorious case. Discussions at that meeting concerned actions black people could take to work for their rights.

Later that year Parks took her momentous action. As her usual bus travelled along its route, all of the white-only seats filled up. The bus reached the third stop in front of the Empire Theatre, and several white passengers boarded. The driver moved the "coloured" section sign back behind Parks and demanded that four black people including Parks give up their seats in the middle section so that the white passengers could sit. Parks had had enough. She said No and was promptly arrested.

Three days later, on Sunday December 4 1955, plans for the Montgomery bus boycott in her support had been announced. The black people of Montgomery had had enough too. At a huge rally that night they agreed to continue the boycott until they were treated with a level of courtesy, until black drivers were hired and until seating in the middle of the bus was handled on a first-come basis.

The next day Parks was tried. The trial lasted just 30 minutes. Found guilty she was fined $10 with $4 costs. Parks appealed and formally challenged the legality of racial segregation. Parks became an icon of the civil rights movement but she also suffered hardships. She was sacked from her job. Her husband quit his job after his boss forbade him to talk about his wife or the legal case. It didn't stop Parks travelling and speaking extensively about the issues.

Later that year, at the urging of her brother and sister-in-law Rosa, Raymond and her mother moved north to Detroit. Parks worked as a seamstress until 1965.

In 1965, John Conyers, an African-American politician hired her as a secretary and receptionist for his congressional office. She held this position until she retired in 1988.

Her husband Raymond died in August 1977. In 1987 she founded the Rosa and Raymond Parks Institute for Self-Development. It runs Pathways to Freedom bus tours which take young people to important civil rights and Underground Railroad sites throughout the country.

When in 1994 the Ku Klux Klan applied to sponsor a portion of United States Interstate 55 at St Louis, Missouri, and the state found that it could not legally refuse the racists' sponsorship, instead it voted to name the highway section the "Rosa Parks Highway."

Rosa Parks died of natural causes at the age of 92 in October 2005. She and her husband never had children. City officials in Montgomery and Detroit announced in a unique tribute that the front seats of all city buses would be reserved with black ribbons in honour of Rosa Parks until her funeral. Her coffin was taken to Washington DC and transported by a bus similar to the one in which she made her protest, to lie in honour in the rotunda of the US Capitol. She was the first woman and only the second black person to lie in state in the Capitol. An estimated 50,000 people viewed the casket there and millions saw it on television.

In later life and after her death Parks received national and international recognition. She was invited to be part of the group welcoming Nelson Mandela upon his release from prison in South Africa. Time magazine named her one of the 20 most influential and iconic figures of the 20th century.

President Bill Clinton awarded her the Presidential Medal of Freedom. She was also presented with the Congressional Gold Medal. Later this month a statue will be unveiled In Washington's Capitol. It will be the first statue of a black woman there. This month all over the US they are celebrating the centenary of this amazing person. We too should pay tribute to Rosa Parks — the woman who sat down for freedom.

ROSA'S WONDERFUL SISTERS

We returned to Rosa Parks and some of her female comrades on December 1 2015 60 years after Rosa Parks refused to give up her seat to white passengers on a segregated bus.

Rosa Parks Rosa Parks refusal to surrender her bus seat to a white passenger 60 years ago spurred the Montgomery boycott and other efforts to end segregation.

She was born in 1913 in Tuskegee, Alabama. After her parents separated Rosa's mother moved the family to live with her parents, Rose and Sylvester Edwards — both former slaves and strong advocates for racial equality.

Among Rosa's early memories was one incident where her grandfather stood in front of their house with a shotgun while Ku Klux Klan members marched down the street.

In 1932, at age 19, Rosa met and married Raymond Parks, an active member of the National Association for the Advancement of Coloured People (NAACP). She became the local NAACP youth leader. Both she and her husband attended Communist Party meetings and schools, completing their political education. By the 1940s she was campaigning on various issues from segregation to white men's sexual abuse of black women.

Then on December 1 1955, after a long day's work as a seamstress at a Montgomery department store, Parks boarded the Cleveland Avenue bus for home. She took a seat in the first of several rows designated for "coloured" passengers. As the bus began to fill with white passengers the driver noticed that several white passengers were standing in the aisle. He stopped the bus and asked four black passengers to give up their seats.

In an action that would change the world, Rosa refused and remained seated. The police arrested Rosa at the scene.

After Parks' heroic action, it was Jo Ann Robinson who organised a city bus boycott by black US citizens in Montgomery, Alabama.

Jo Ann Gibson Robinson

Born in 1912 in Georgia, she was the 12th child of her farmer parents. She became the first college graduate of her family. Becoming a school teacher in 1949, Robinson moved to Montgomery to teach English at Alabama State College.

She also became active in the Montgomery community, joining the Women's Political Council (WPC), a group designed to motivate black women to take political action.

In the late 1940s she was screamed at for sitting in the empty white section of a city bus. This incident led her to start to fight against the segregated city bus system. When Robinson became president of the WPC in 1950, she focused the organisation's efforts to desegregate buses. Following the arrest of Parks on December 1 1955, Robinson urged Montgomery's black residents to boycott city buses on December 5 of that year.

When the boycott proved successful, many male leaders of the civil rights movement including Martin Luther King Junior moved in to take over leadership of the campaign, but Robinson was appointed to the executive board and produced a weekly newsletter at King's personal request.

For her role as a leader of the boycott, Robinson was arrested and targeted with violence. Police officers threw a rock into her window and poured acid on her car.

Daisy Bates

Born in November 1914 her birth mother had been raped and murdered by three local white men. Bates was raised by foster parents.

In 1941 she and her husband started one of the first newspapers specifically for black people. Her Arkansas State Press carried stories about civil rights and became an early voice for black protest.

Daisy became a leader in the fight to desegregate Arkansas schools. Her house became a meeting place where black children assembled to march to school, often with Daisy leading them.

These daily processions were attacked both by local racists and state troopers. The children were turned away from the whites-only schools but the battle went on.

The Ku Klux Klan planted blazing crosses outside Daisy's house on more than one occasion.

In 1954 the Supreme Court made all the segregated schools illegal, but still the schools in Arkansas refused to enrol black students.

In 1957, because of its strong voice during the Little Rock schools campaign, white advertisers boycotted Daisy's paper. This successfully cut off funding and the paper was forced to close in October 1959.

Daisy Bates continued to campaign with the NAACP and her work made a huge contribution to the final victory in desegregating education all across the South.

Ruby Hurley

She was born in Virginia in 1909, during the period of racist Jim Crow laws. In 1939 she was involved in organising a concert by black singer Marian Anderson. The racist Daughters of the American Revolution tried to ban the concert.

Ruby arranged for Anderson to perform on the steps of the Lincoln Memorial to a live audience of over 75,000 and a radio audience of millions.

In 1943 she became youth secretary of the NAACP. She would work for them for over 40 years.

She moved to Birmingham, Alabama, where she opened the first permanent NAACP office in the Deep South. She investigated beatings, lynchings and judicial murders, including the cases of the Rev George Lee and Emmett Till, both in 1955, and Medgar Evers in 1963.

At the time of Hurley's achievements the NAACP and the civil rights movement were still largely dominated by men. She is hugely admired as a pioneer of black feminist activism.

Amelia Boynton Robinson

She was born in 1911 in Savannah, Georgia. Both of her parents were of African-American, Cherokee Indian and German descent. Her early activism included holding black voter registration drives. She came to world prominence when she was brutally beaten while leading a 1965 civil rights march in Selma, Alabama.

In 1964 she ran on the Democratic ticket for a seat in Congress from Alabama, becoming the first black woman to do so, as well as the first woman to run as a Democratic candidate for Congress in Alabama. She died in August this year at the age of 104.

Fannie Lou Hamer

Born in 1917 in the Mississippi Delta, she was the youngest of 20 children in a sharecropping family. At the age of six she started work picking cotton. During surgery to remove a tumour she was given an unauthorised hysterectomy, a common practice to sterilise young poor black women.

In 1962 she met civil rights activists who encouraged blacks to register to vote. That year she travelled with 17 others to the county courthouse in Indianola to register. All along the way the bus was attacked by local and state law enforcement.

She encouraged her fellow campaigners by singing hymns. It would become her trademark tactic in future protests. For having the audacity to try to register to vote, Fannie was fired from her job and driven from her plantation home.

From then on Fannie dedicated her life to the fight for civil rights, working for the Student Nonviolent Co-ordinating Committee. She was threatened, arrested, beaten, and shot at. In 1964, she helped found the Mississippi Freedom Democratic Party.

Fannie Hamer died in 1977. Her grave carries one of her best quotes: "I am sick and tired of being sick and tired."

A SACRIFICE MADE FOR US ALL

EMILY WILDING DAVISON

Published June 6 2013, the centenary of Emily's death under the king's horse at the Derby.

In the quiet churchyard of St Mary the Virgin, Morpeth, Northumberland, there is a white gravestone with an inspiring message. "Deeds not words," it says. This is the final resting place of working-class hero and martyr, the suffragette Emily Wilding Davison, who died a century ago tomorrow.

On June 4 1913 she leapt in front of the King's horse running in the Derby. That protest, demanding votes for women, cost Davison her life. The Morpeth tomb is not the only memorial to this remarkable woman. On April 2 1911, the night of the 1911 census, Davison hid in a cupboard in the Palace of Westminster. That way she could legitimately give her place of residence on census night as the House of Commons. Census documents record that Emily Wilding Davison was found hiding in the crypt in the Houses of Parliament. In 1999 Tony Benn, against much opposition, placed a plaque to commemorate the event in a Westminster broom cupboard (with the help of a certain Jeremy Corbyn MP).

Emily Davison was born in Blackheath, London. Both parents were from Northumberland. She attended Kensington High School and won a bursary to Royal Holloway College in 1891 to study literature. Just a year into her studies her father died and her recently widowed mother could not afford the £20-a-term fees. Davison found jobs, first as a private governess, then as a teacher. She saved enough to study biology, chemistry, English language and literature at St Hugh's College, Oxford, where she obtained a first-class honours degree. She went on to obtain another first-class honours degree from London University.

In 1906 she joined the Women's Social and Political Union (WSPU).

Formed in 1903 by Emmeline Pankhurst, the WSPU brought together those who felt strongly that only militant, direct action would win women the vote.

In 1908, Davison left her teaching post to dedicate herself full-time to the suffragette movement. She became a militant and effective campaigner disrupting meetings, throwing stones and even trying her hand at arson.

On nine occasions she was arrested and imprisoned for various offences. In prison she went on hunger strike and was force-fed. In June 1912, near the end of a six-month sentence in Holloway Prison for arson, she protested at fellow suffragettes being force-fed by throwing herself down a 30-foot iron staircase. As a result she suffered severe head and spinal damage, causing her pain for the rest of her life.

On Derby day — June 4 1913 — she carried out her most famous and tragically fatal protest. There is some evidence that she didn't mean to kill herself. She had bought a return ticket and sent postcards to friends arranging future meetings. It may be she was trying to attach a suffragette flag to Anmer, the King's horse, so that when the horse crossed the finishing line, it would be flying the WSPU flag. Two such flags were found on her body.

Pathé News captured the incident on film. The film, which can be seen on the internet to this day, shows Davison stepping out onto the racecourse just as the leading horses sweep by. The film is unclear but it is possible she had taken the banner of the WSPU out from where it was concealed in her clothing. The horse knocked her to the ground unconscious. She died in hospital four days later.

Herbert Jones, the jockey who was riding the horse, suffered a mild concussion in the incident. In 1928, at the funeral of Emmeline Pankhurst, the jockey Jones laid a wreath "to do honour to the memory of Mrs Pankhurst and Miss Emily Davison."

Next time you meet someone who tells you they haven't bothered to use their vote, remind them that people died to get them that right. And one of them was the very brave Emily Wilding Davison.

REAL HEROES REMEMBERED — MUCH TOO LATE

VIOLETTE SZABO, ANDREE BORREL, LISE DE BAISSAC, YOLANDE BEEKMAN AND NANCY WAKE

Published on December 5 2013 when Prince Charles and the British Establishment finally marked some remarkable heroism 70 years before in the battle to defeat the nazis.

On Tuesday this week in Bedfordshire, Prince Charles finally unveiled a memorial to honour and remember the brave women who flew out of RAF Tempsford to aid resistance movements in occupied Europe during the second world war. The unveiling marks the end of an almost year-long campaign to set up the Tempsford memorial. This means that at last there is a fitting tribute to some of the wonderful women agents who flew on those secret missions from this Bedfordshire field.

Some 80-odd women agents left the small airfield. They worked as radio operators, couriers, and in many other roles. All of them were also trained in military skills and in spycraft. They worked with the Free French forces as well as the many French communists who played such an important part in the French Resistance. Between them they won nearly 100 high commendations including Four George Crosses — the highest British civilian honour — one George medal, one CBE, 16 MBEs and four OBEs. There were French awards too, including 27 Croix de Guerre and 10 Legion d'Honneur.

The first to go were two young women, Andree Borrel, codename Denise, and Lise De Baissac, codename Odile, who flew out on the night of September 24 1942. Yolande Beekman, codename Marriette, had married just a month before she was flown out from RAF Tempsford on September 18 1943. She worked as a wireless operator for Gustave Bieler, the head of the Musician Network in the St Quentin district of Belgium. After many close escapes she and Bieler were finally captured by the Germans on January 12 1944.

Bieler was shot soon after capture by the SS at Flossenberg. Beekman, however, was brutally tortured during Gestapo interrogation. Like so many of her comrades she said nothing. Beekman was executed at Dachau concentration camp on September 12 1944 aged 32.

Australian Nancy Wake married a French businessman in 1939 and fled France when the Germans invaded in 1940. Back in England she joined the Special Operations Executive (SOE). There was no moon on April 28 1944 so her flight into occupied France from Tempsford had to be postponed until the next night. The next night she parachuted into the Auvergne district of France to help the French rise up on D-Day.

Another airfield with a similar story is just off the A14 at junction three in Northamptonshire. It stands behind a scruffy lay-by in front of a huge field. In the lay-by is a memorial to the "801/492 US-AAF squadron." This memorial also carries a more romantic message. "Harrington airfield," it tells you, "was home to the Carpetbaggers."

So who were these strangely named bands of heroes? Fortunately a tiny but packed museum just down the lane tells the full and fascinating story. The Carpetbaggers were the US flyers that secretly supplied the French Resistance with all they needed for their heroic war work of spying and sabotage. Every moonlit night a couple of dozen black painted and unmarked B24 bombers would take off for France.

The bays would be full of parachute canisters, boxes and baskets of weapons and ammunition, civilian clothes, counterfeit nazi uniforms, radio sets, even bicycles — the one-hundred-and-one things the French Resistance needed to carry on their essential but dangerous work behind nazi lines.

The BBC would broadcast to France coded messages identifying the drop zones. The Carpetbaggers would fly low over occupied France avoiding anti-aircraft fire to drop their parachutes. And as if this wasn't heroic enough some nights the cargo was even more precious, even more secret. It was from Harrington too that the brave men and women agents were flown into France under the noses of the enemy. Their average life expectancy was just three months.

Perhaps the best known was Violette Szabo. So secret were the exploits of the agents that we still don't know which routes she used to enter France. Szabo started the war on the perfume counter of the Bon Marche store in Brixton. Her mother was French, her father a London cabbie. She joined the undercover SOE and carried out three dangerous operations to occupied France.

After training by the SOE she was dropped into occupied France three times. The best evidence suggests she flew out of both Tempsford and later from Harrington. Just four days after her last landing in France on June 10 1944 she was ambushed near Limoges by the nazis. Cornered, wounded and alone, she fought off the crack Geman SS troops with her machine gun until her ammunition was exhausted. Despite brutal torture and interrogation she gave nothing away. Sent to Ravensbruck concentration camp, she was eventually shot on January 25 1945. She was just 23 years old.

You may have seen the film Carve Her Name With Pride. It tells the story of one of these brave female French agents like Szabo far better than I could. Many of these heroes were sadly, like her, never to return.

But we owe them all an enormous debt of gratitude for the contribution they made to the defeat of fascism. And now, after 70 years, it seems our government is belatedly paying tribute too. Now at last Szabo and her comrades have the memorial they have long deserved.

Visit www.harringtonmuseum.org.uk and www.tempsford.20m. com for more details.

A COUNTESS NEVER TO BE FORGOTTEN

COUNTESS CONSTANCE MARKIEVICZ

Published in the Christmas Edition 2013 after a question in a pub quiz reawakened memories of an English aristocrat who played a momentous part in Irish working-class history.

"**W**e was robbed!" The Christmas quiz at the village pub is a key fixture for my quiz team, "The Comrades." We were doing well, in equal first place, and when Harry the quizmaster declared the tie-breaker round would be on British politics. We knew we were home and dry. It was neck and neck on the first nine questions and then came the final decider. Harry asked it: "Who was the first ever woman elected to the House of Commons, and in what year?" "Easy," said the other team. It's an old favourite pub quiz question. We let them go first. As we expected they answered: "Viscountess Nancy Astor in 1919."

We knew we'd won. The correct answer was, as any good republican knows, "Countess Constance Markievicz in 1918." Elected for Sinn Fein in Dublin South, like the other 72 republicans voted in she would not pledge allegiance to the king and never took her seat. But elected to the House of Commons she certainly was, 95 years ago this very month.

Then quizmaster Harry pronounced his verdict. "Lady Astor, Tory and Unionist MP for Plymouth in 1919 — correct." He was wrong of course, but have you ever met a pub quizmaster who admitted he was wrong?

Poor Countess Constance Markievicz, hated by the British Establishment from which she sprang, has always been sidelined by history and never received the credit she so richly deserves. Not on this side of the Irish Sea anyway.

Countess Constance was: elected to Parliament while serving a prison sentence; first ever woman elected to Westminster in 1918; first ever woman elected to the Dail Eireann, the Irish parliament; first ever female minister in any government anywhere in the world as Irish minister of labour from 1919-22; and first female Irish cabinet minister.

And she achieved a score of other important firsts for women and in Irish politics.

What a woman. She and her sister Eva were courted by Ireland's greatest poet William Butler Yeats. Both sisters turned down Yeats's proposals of marriage. Constance would become companion, comrade and sometimes lover to some of Ireland's greatest heroes including James Connolly, Jim Larkin, Michael Collins and Eamon de Valera.

She was born in 1868 as Constance Georgina Gore-Booth in London into a wealthy family that had a large estate at Lissadell in Co Sligo. Her father, Sir Henry Gore-Booth, was an explorer, but unlike many landowners in Ireland he treated his tenants fairly and well, providing free food in the 1879-90 famine for instance.

Both sisters were debutantes, presented to Queen Victoria. Both could have chosen an easy life as part of the aristocracy. Neither did. Sister Eva became part of the labour movement in England and a keen suffragette. Constance too joined the campaign for votes for women. Eva would campaign against the first world war and join the Independent Labour Party and play her part in many other peace, trade union, feminist and socialist groups.

Constance, less politically active at the time, studied art at the Slade and in Paris where she met and married Count Casimir Markievicz. In 1903 the couple moved to Dublin and the countess gained a reputation for herself as a landscape artist. She also acted at the Abbey Theatre.

She joined the revolutionary group The Daughters of Ireland. Although turning up at her first meeting in a satin ball gown and a diamond tiara didn't do her any favours, she had come direct from a grand government ball.

In 1906 she rented a small cottage in the countryside close to Dublin. The previous tenant had left behind old copies of The Peasant and Sinn Fein, a revolutionary publication that argued for freedom from British rule. The countess read these fascinating old documents and the ideas she discovered in them changed her life forever.

By 1908 she was deeply involved in nationalist politics in Ireland. She joined Sinn Fein and Inghinidhe na hEireann, a militant republican women's movement. In that year, she first stood for Parliament, unsuccessfully standing against Winston Churchill in Manchester.

In 1909 she founded the youth movement Fianna Eireann. They were effectively republican and paramilitary-armed Boy and Girl Scouts. The Fianna taught teenagers to shoot as well as Irish history and radical republican politics. Padraig Pearse would credit Fianna Eireann as important to the foundation of the Irish Volunteers in 1913.

In 1911 Markievicz was jailed for the first time. She had demonstrated against the visit of George V. They arrested her when she publicly burned the union flag.

In the Dublin lockout of 1913, alongside James Connolly, James Larkin and Maud Gonne she ran a soup kitchen in Liberty Hall to aid those strikers who could not afford food. Constance sold her jewellery to pay for the food. No wonder she was elected treasurer of James Connolly's Irish Citizen Army.

She designed her own stylish Citizen Army uniform in rich green Irish linen with a dramatic cocked hat sporting long red feathers. She could not resist having an old friend, a society photographer, take some startling pictures of her in uniform posing with her long-barrelled revolver.

In the Easter Rising of 1916 her distinctive uniform became well known as she played a very active role in the street fighting in central Dublin. She was second in command at St Stephen's Green and held out against the British army for six days, conceding defeat only when shown the surrender order signed by Pearse himself.

She was paraded through the streets of Dublin with other arrested leaders and then held in solitary confinement at Kilmainham Gaol.

The British courts martial sentenced her to death. They commuted her sentence because she was a woman. Markievicz was angry at this special treatment. She protested: "I do wish your lot had the decency to shoot me."

The British court had no mercy on her male comrades — the leaders were all shot. The injured Connolly, unable to stand, was shot tied in a chair.

She was released from prison in 1917 but not for long. By 1918 she was jailed again for her part in anti-conscription activities. It was during this sentence that she won her seat in Westminster's House of Commons.

In the civil war she was a staunch opponent of the 1921 treaty which gave Ireland dominion status within the British empire. Michael Collins, the man who signed the treaty, claimed that his old comrade Constance could never understand the rationale behind the treaty as she was English. She called him a traitor. After the civil war ended, she toured the United States.

The countess was also re-elected to the Dail but her staunch republican views led her to being sent to jail yet again. In prison she and 92 other female prisoners went on hunger strike. Within a month the countess was released. The hunger strikes of the suffragettes had been a huge embarrassment to the British government before the war. The newly created Dail could not afford a similar scandal.

In 1926 the republican movement split. Markievicz joined Fianna Fail, led by Eamonn de Valera. Just five weeks later she was dead of tuberculosis contracted while working in the poorhouses of Dublin.

Over a quarter of a million Irish people lined the streets as her funeral made its way to the republican plot at Glasnevin Cemetery. Ireland has never forgotten Countess Constance Markievicz and it never will, even if our quizmaster Harry has.

THE REAL SALLY BOWLES
JEAN ROSS

*Published December 31 2013 to celebrate a mysterious woman
I met in the Communist Party half a century before.*

When I first joined the Young Communist League in the early 1960s I met some amazing people. One was Joe Bent, a well-known and leading communist in community politics in Southwark, south-east London. Bent was a regular communist candidate in many elections. In one Greater London Council election he narrowly missed winning a seat by fewer than 1,000 votes. He was a great speaker and would come to talk at our YCL meetings.

When he did he was often accompanied by an elegant and fascinating women comrade. Her name was Jean Ross. Ross lived in Barnes, west London, and had a large Daily Worker round among her neighbours. She also helped Bent in his many election and other campaigns.

When the film Cabaret was released in 1972 I first heard a strange and at the time, almost unbelievable story. That same Jean Ross, it was said, was the real Sally Bowles, chief character in the film played by Liza Minnelli.

Ross died in 1973 and I was never able to track down the origins or indeed the veracity of the stories. Now, 40 years after her death, I think I've found the truth. It is certainly an amazing tale and one worth telling.

Her full name it seems was Jean Iris Ross. She was born in Alexandria, Egypt, in 1911. Her Scottish father was in the cotton business. Jean was the oldest of four children. She was shipped back to England to be educated. She hated her school. She was bright and had done all the sixth-form work by the time she was 16. Bored stiff, she feigned pregnancy to get herself expelled.

In desperation her parents tried sending her to finishing school in Switzerland. That didn't last long either. Using a small allowance from her grandfather Ross took herself to the Royal Academy of Dramatic Art, where despite winning a prize for acting she left after just one year. In 1930, aged just 19, she got her first film part, playing a harem woman in low-budget and long-forgotten film When Sailors Leave Home.

Ross and another young actor friend heard there were jobs for young actors in Germany. The pair set off for Berlin. No acting jobs materialised but Ross did find work as a fashion magazine model. That was the day job. In the evening she sang in the many Berlin cabaret clubs.

In 1931 young British writer Christopher Isherwood was soaking up the atmosphere of those clubs. Isherwood and Ross became close friends and even shared lodgings. Isherwood based the heroine of his book Sally Bowles on Ross and her life in Berlin. He also made her the chief character in his later book Goodbye to Berlin.

In Berlin a botched abortion nearly took her life. The baby's father was a musician called Goetz von Eick. He would become well known in Hollywood as Peter van Eyck.

Ross was on holiday in England when Hitler and his nazis took power. She saw the writing on the wall and decided not to return to Germany. That nazi warning inspired her to join the Communist Party in Chelsea. She remained a communist till the day she died.

In England her career was going well, with stage parts and modelling for magazines like Tatler. Her fluency in German and her knowledge of the German entertainment world found her work in a British film industry newly populated with German and Austrian film directors fleeing nazi persecution. One was Berthold Viertel, who was making a film of Ernst Lothar's novel Little Friend. Ross suggested her old pal Isherwood as a script writer.

As well as being the original Sally Bowles, Ross was also remembered in another piece of popular culture. Eric Maschwitz's popular song These Foolish Things Remind Me of You was based on Ross. She and the married Maschwitz had an affair and the song is a lasting memorial to that flirtation.

Ross was always elegant and stylish, right up to her death. She usually carried a long black silver-tipped cane — perhaps unusual for a communist. One night in the Cafe Royal — then a meeting place for London's bohemians — she met Claud Cockburn. Cockburn asked her to cash a cheque but phoned her the next day to tell her it would bounce. Strangely that didn't end the friendship before it started. At the time Cockburn was employed by the Daily Worker, forerunner of today's Morning Star. The two became firm friends and soon lovers. They would sit up till the early hours of the morning discussing Marxist economics.

Cockburn suggested Ross should become a journalist. She did and got a job as a reporter on the Daily Express. The couple were on holiday in Spain when the civil war broke out. They both stayed on, she reporting for the Express, he for the Worker. When Cockburn went to fight with the International Brigades, Ross wrote his reports for him. She sent stories to the Daily Worker under his name and in his style, and filed her own, very different, copy to the Express. Later she would become both a reporter and also a film critic for the Daily Worker.

In 1937 Ross and Cockburn, now living together in south London, had a daughter Sarah. The couple never married and three months after Sarah was born Cockburn walked out never to return. Ross and young Sarah moved away from London as the bombs started falling — first to Hertfordshire and then to Cheltenham. Ross wanted Sarah to have a Scottish education so they moved north of the border. In 1960 Ross moved back to south London where she settled in Barnes.

Daughter Sarah went to Oxford University and became a very successful writer of detective stories and a notable pipe-smoker.

Ross concentrated on work for the Communist Party and the Daily Worker. The media would frequently come seeking out the real Sally Bowles. Sarah recalled: "Journalists always wanted to talk about sex and my mother always wanted to talk about politics."

Ross died, aged 62, 40 years ago in 1973 at her home in Barnes.

She may have been the inspiration for the well remembered Sally, but in many ways the story of Jean Ross's rich life is much more fascinating than any character in any work of fiction.

MORE THAN MR MARIE LLOYD

MARIE LLOYD

Published January 10 2014 this article pays tribute to music hall star Alec Hurley who died almost exactly 100 years before and his wife Marie Lloyd.

Some remember Alec Hurley, who died 100 years ago in November 1913 only as 'Mr Marie Lloyd'. In fact he deserves to be remembered in his own right, both as a popular and talented performer and as a pioneer of workers' rights.

In his teens Alec, a merchant seaman's son from the East End, had given up his job as a tea-packer and taken to the stage. By the time he was 20, in 1891, Hurley was already topping the bill. Then he met perhaps the greatest music hall star — Marie Lloyd. Marie was already married but that didn't stop her and Alec falling in love and soon moving in together.

They became a double act. In 1901, the pair toured Australia with huge success. Marie divorced in 1905, allowing her and Alec to marry in 1906. The couple shared strong socialist political principles. Together they would make an immense contribution to trade union organisation among stage performers. The couple's Hampstead home became a place for militant performers to meet, discuss and organise.

Marie had a well known reputation for songs and stories told of the hardships of working-class life, especially for working-class women. Her risqué interpretations of the most innocent of lyrics led to frequent clashes with the establishment. When her song She Sits Among the Cabbages and Peas was banned she simply sang: "She sits among the cabbages and leeks."

Despite her and Alec's own success and relatively high pay the two of them had always supported other performers as passionate trade unionists. Fellow female artistes voted Marie as the first president of the Music Hall Ladies Guild in 1906. In the following year she and Alec called a meeting to form an industry alliance. The National Association of Theatrical Employees and the Amalgamated Musicians Union joined with the Variety Artists Federation (VAF). The VAF still exists as part of the actors' union Equity.

The VAF took strike action in 1907 to resist greedy music hall management attempts to make lesser known artists do unpaid extra matinee performances and to cut wages and perks. Marie and Alec, as top-bill performers were not directly affected by these worsening conditions, but they threw their weight behind the strike. Meetings were held in their home and the couple also made major financial contributions to strike funds.

One strike breaker was Belle Elmore, a decidedly second-rate performer who was later murdered by her famous husband Dr Crippen. Elmore crossed the picket line. Strikers told Elmore not to be a blackleg. Marie, who thought little of Elmore's talent, shouted: "Let her through, girls, she'll close the music hall faster than we can." As Elmore came on stage, strikers told the audience that Marie Lloyd was singing for free on the picket line outside. The theatre emptied. The strike was won.

Sadly by 1910, Marie's increasing drinking and infidelities had put a real strain on her relationship with Hurley. She had met a young Irish jockey. He was 22 and Marie was 40; she moved in with him, leaving Alec to tour and live alone.

Hurley however remained popular both on and off stage. But it was a life cut tragically short. In Glasgow on Friday November 28 1913, Alec was taken ill on stage. He died of pneumonia just a week later. He was just 42. The stage had lost a great performer but wages, conditions and trade union organisation in the entertainment industry would never be the same again.

Marie remained true to her political principles and suffered for it. When the first-ever royal command performance was organised in 1912, Marie's left-wing anti-Establishment views ensured she was excluded. Marie hired a nearby theatre on the same night. Placards proclaimed: "Every performance by Marie Lloyd is a command performance — by command of the British public."

In 1922, aged just 52, Marie gave her final performance at the Edmonton Empire music hall. She collapsed on stage during one of her best known numbers One of the Ruins Cromwell Knocked About A Bit. As she staggered all over the stage the audience thought it part of the show and laughed and applauded. Marie died a few days later. Fifty-thousand people attended her Hampstead funeral.

FORGET LORD KITCHENER, CAVELL IS THE REAL HERO

EDITH CAVELL

Published January 13 2014 when the Royal Mint announced that Lord Kitchener would appear on the new £2 commemorative coin.

I'm not sure who is the most insensitive, Education Minister Michael Gove or the Royal Mint. It isn't just those of us on the left who see the slaughter of the first world war as lions led by donkeys. The history of insensitive and incompetent officers, the donkeys, sending brave men to an unnecessary early death are well documented in Establishment histories as well as Oh What a Lovely War and Blackadder Goes Forth.

Now the Royal Mint is planning to honour one of the most insensitive of the donkeys. Lord Kitchener convinced thousands of working-class lads to sign up. We shouldn't forget that many very young lads lied about their age to answer Kitchener's jingoistic appeal. Quite simply Kitchener was a warmonger with the blood of millions on his hands.

Even before WWI he had a reputation for atrocities. He led the Omdurman massacre in Sudan in 1898 and expanded the network of concentration camps in South Africa. Many civilians died in the unhealthy conditions. No wonder there has been a huge campaign to stop the issuing of the new Kitchener coin, over 20,000 people have added their names to a petition seeking to do just that.

I think a coin to mark WWI would actually be a good idea but can I suggest a much more suitable candidate as the hero who should be on the coin? My candidate for the coin is nurse Edith Cavell. The message on the coin her famous last words; "Patriotism is not enough, I must have no hatred or bitterness towards anyone."

I'm not the only one backing Edith Cavell for the new WWI coin there is already an online petition with thousands of signatures. Sioned-Mair Richards, a Labour city councillor in Sheffield, who launched the petition, told us: "It's really struck a chord with people," she said. Ms Richards a former mayor of Carmarthen, said she had admired Cavell since she was a girl. "Lord Kitchener represents all that I have always loathed about the first world war — the jingoism, the sheer waste of men, the 'lions led by donkeys' mentality," she said. "And then I thought of Edith Cavell, a heroine of my early childhood. The nurse who was executed for giving succour to all wounded soldiers regardless of nationality."

Edith Cavell was a vicar's daughter, an English matron of a teaching hospital in Belgium. She had already built a huge reputation as an influential pioneer of modern nursing. When World War I broke out she was visiting her mother in Norfolk. She hurried back to Belgium where she knew her nursing skills would be urgently needed.

Edith's hospital became a Red Cross station for wounded soldiers. She ensured all nationalities were equally treated in her wards. "I can't stop while there are lives to be saved" she said. When a number of wounded British soldiers, cut off from their comrades, arrived at the hospital, Edith faced a dilemma.

Should she help the British soldiers and put at risk the neutrality of the Red Cross and endanger those working with her? If she refused to help the soldiers they would be in danger of being shot, along with any Belgian civilians who had harboured them.

Edith decided to help them despite the risk to herself. "Had I not helped, they would have been shot," she later said. In order to help them she joined the Belgian underground. Her actions helped more than 200 Allied soldiers to escape to neutral territory.

When the network was betrayed, Edith was arrested, found guilty of treason by a court martial, and sentenced to death. Cavell was shot, in her nurse's uniform, by a firing squad, at dawn on October 12 1915, in Brussels.

On the eve of her execution she uttered the words that will always be linked with her name and her bravery. "I realise that patriotism is not enough, I must have no hatred or bitterness towards anyone."

SHE INVENTED THE DRAMA DOCUMENTARY

KAY MANDER

Obituary published January 23 2014.

F ilm-maker Kay Mander who almost single handedly invented the drama documentary has died aged 98. She got interested in film-making while living in Germany. She worked as a translator at the 1935 Berlin International Film Congress.

Back in Britain she found work at Alexander Korda's London Films as an interpreter. Here she worked in publicity and continuity becoming one of the first women members of the film union ACC&T.

Her big break came during the second world war when many experienced male colleagues joined the armed services. She was offered a job as a production assistant at the Shell Film Unit. It was here she made her directing debut.

Her first short film, made in 1941, on the dry subject of how to file metal was made to instruct young unskilled women entering engineering and munitions factories. She produced a seven-minute work of art and won its young director much acclaim in the industry.

By 1943 Mander was turning out home-front propaganda films on subjects like the fire service and civil defence. However mundane the subject her direction both bought humanity and got its message over.

In 1943 she was invited to make a simple documentary about the government-subsidised Highland and Islands Medical Service. Instead she scripted, produced, directed and even acted in, one of the first ever drama documentaries. The film Highland Doctor used professional actors and local people to bring a dramatic story and the ideal alive. The film was not only popular and successful but it was also one of the most powerful arguments in the battle to promote the socialist ideal of a National Health Service.

While shooting Highland Doctor in the Highlands and Western

Isles she fell in love with Scotland, where she eventually chose to live. Peace saw many male film-makers back from the war and her work started to dry up. Perhaps it didn't help that she was a deeply committed and outspoken member of the Communist Party and made no attempt to hide her political views in her work. In the 1945 film Homes for the People, for instance, she had ordinary, working-class women speak bluntly about lousy housing.

At this time Mander and her husband, the documentary producer RK Neilson-Baxter were shooting educational and promotional films for government and industrial sponsors. In 1949 her French-language films for the Ministry of Education La Famille Martin won a British Film Academy Award. After the war she and her husband lived and worked briefly in Asia. Back in Scotland in 1957 she wrote and directed one feature for the Children's Film Foundation, The Kid from Canada (1957). She didn't want to make children's, or indeed women's, films and mainstream director's roles were becoming harder to find. So she started to work on big Hollywood films but in the less glamorous continuity department.

She worked on a huge range of movies including From Russia with Love The Four Horsemen of the Apocalypse , Fahrenheit 451, Tommy and the Heroes of Telemark. On the set of Telemark she met and had a brief affair with star Kirk Douglas.

She knew he had a terrible reputation "He flew his ladies in first-class, kept them for a long weekend, and sent them back economy." She would wistfully remember later. Despite this, and despite the hurt it caused her husband, she took the initiative and instigated a brief affair with Douglas.

In 1978, she moved permanently north of the border to a chalet on a farm outside Dumfries. Today critics and historians have recognised Kay Mander's importance, both as a pioneering woman film-maker and as a brilliant documentary maker. Her invention, the drama documentary has become a major weapon in the radical film-maker's arsenal.

A documentary — One Continuous Take — was made about her in 2001 and a boxed set of her work released in 2010. Both are available on DVD.

WHEN HITLER'S PERFECT WOMAN CAME TO LONDON

GERTRUD SCHOLTZ-KLINK

Published April 2 2014 75 years after British appeasers and nazi sympathisers tried a clever propaganda move. This woman is no hero.

Seventy-five years ago in 1939, as war clouds gathered over Europe, a German woman Hitler had described as the "perfect nazi female" arrived in London. When Adolf Hitler came to power in 1933 he appointed long-time nazi supporter Gertrud Scholtz-Klink as Reich's Women's Fuehrerin and head of the Nazi Women's League.

Ironically, Scholtz-Klink argued against the participation of women in politics. "Anyone who has seen the communist women scream on the street and in parliament realise that such an activity is not something which is done by a true woman," she declared.

By July 1936 Scholtz-Klink was appointed head of the Women's Bureau in the German Labour Front. Her job was to encourage women to work for the nazi government.

On the face of it the Fuehrerin's visit to London was at the invitation of Prunella Stack, leader of the Women's League of Health and Beauty, an early women's keep-fit organisation with nearly 200,000 members all across Britain and the empire. Stack, still only 25, had inherited the well-paid top position in this commercially successful organisation on the death of her mother, the league's founder Mary Bagot-Stack.

Prunella Stack had married Lord David Douglas-Hamilton, who was part of a well-known right-wing family. Her brother-in-law, a Tory MP and well-known nazi sympathiser, the 14th Duke of Hamilton, had attended the 1936 nazi Olympics in Berlin. While there he dined with Joachim von Ribbentrop, an old friend. Ribbentrop was the German ambassador to Britain and later Hitler's foreign minister.

In Berlin the duke met Hitler and many other leading nazis. With Hermann Goering he inspected the rapidly growing Luftwaffe. During this visit it is probable that he first made contact with Rudolf Hess.

It was Hess who, on May 10 1941, parachuted into Scotland to meet the duke and plot a secret peace treaty that would lead to the supremacy of Germany within Europe alongside a strengthened British empire. Hess crash-landed and ended up in hospital. Hamilton rushed to his bedside and contacted Winston Churchill to tell him of the deputy fuhrer's arrival. Churchill wanted nothing to do with the traitorous plot. Hess was imprisoned until the end of the war and finally tried at the subsequent Nuremberg trials. He finally hanged himself in Spandau prison in 1987 at the age of 93.

Members of the British Establishment, many of them with their own skeleton-filled cupboards, rallied round to defend Tory Hamilton. The official whitewash declared "the conduct of the Duke of Hamilton has been in every respect honourable and proper."

Stack had taken a troop of her league members to a nazi-organised international congress of physical fitness in Hamburg in 1938. This was a chance for Hitler to show off his nazi "strength through joy" physical fitness movement.

Encouraged by her right-wing friends, appeasers and out-and-out nazis, Stack invited Reichsfrauenfuehrerin Scholtz-Klink to come to London. The Anglo-German Fellowship organised a grand dinner in her honour at Claridges. Members included Bank of England directors Frank Cyril Tiarks and Montagu Norman, Admiral Sir Barry Domvile, Prince von Bismarck and Geoffrey Dawson, editor of the Times. Corporate members included PriceWaterhouse, Unilever, Dunlop Rubber, Thomas Cook, the Midland Bank and Lazard Brothers, among others.

Many Conservative MPs were members, and from the House of Lords came Lord Brocket, Lord Galloway, the Earl of Glasgow, Lord Londonderry, Lord Nuffield, Lord Redesdale, Lord Rennell and the 5th Duke of Wellington.

Scholtz-Klink also used the visit to meet nazi sympathisers who were engaged in secret talks that would result in the foundation of the Right Club, as well as more openly fascist members of the Nordic League. The Right Club was officially founded in May 1939 to rid the Conservative Party of perceived Jewish control.

Its founder was Tory MP Archibald Ramsay. He boasted that "the main objective was to oppose and expose the activities of organised Jewry." Right Club members included William Joyce — aka Lord Haw-Haw — who would broadcast for Hitler in the war.

The Duke of Wellington took the chair at meetings. The club's badge was of an eagle killing a snake with the initials PJ standing for "Perish Judah."

A heroic Daily Worker (forerunner of today's Morning Star) reporter managed to infiltrate a Nordic League meeting at the Wigmore Hall in Marylebone, London. He reported Ramsay as saying that they needed to end Jewish control, "and if we don't do it constitutionally, we'll do it with steel" — a statement greeted with wild applause by fellow fascists.

After the visit and all those meetings, Scholtz-Klink returned to Germany to be at Hitler's side. Just a few days later the nazis invaded Czechoslovakia and within months all Europe was at war.

MOTHER JONES A BYWORD FOR LEFT-WING OPINION IN THE US

MARY HARRIS

Published April 19 2014 as part of a larger feature marking the centenary of the Ludlow Massacre an attack by the Colorado National Guard and Colorado Fuel & Iron Company camp guards on a tent colony of 1,200 striking coalminers and their families at Ludlow, Colorado. Some two dozen people, including miners' wives and children, were killed.

Mother Jones was simply one of the most famous US female labour leaders of the 19th century. Indeed the term "Mother Jones" is still a byword for left-wing opinion in the US. She played a key part in events at Ludlow.

Mary Harris fled famine struck Ireland with her family. She became a teacher and then a seamstress in Chicago. In Memphis in 1861 she married George Jones, an ironworker. George introduced her to the embryonic US labour movement. The couple had four children before the 1867 yellow fever epidemic killed both husband and children. Mary would wear nothing but black for the rest of her life. She moved to work in the sewing sweatshops of Chicago, but again disaster struck and she lost everything in the great Chicago fire of 1871. Rather than mourn, she plunged herself into trade union work, joining the Knights of Labour. From then on she dedicated herself to improving life for working people.

The US had discovered rampant and aggressive capitalism. The greedy few became obscenely rich while more and more US citizens, many recent immigrants, found themselves dirt poor with low wages and long hours — if they could find a job at all. Unemployment stalked the land. Workers had no union rights, no pensions, no healthcare, working conditions were appalling.

The bosses used private armies or state militias to stop workers coming together in a union. Brave organisers like Mother Jones, Joe Hill, Elizabeth Gurley Flynn and many more roamed the country spreading confidence and political understanding among the workers involved in strikes and struggles.

Bear in mind that many of the key working-class organisations did not exist at this time. The Industrial Workers of the World, the famous Wobblies, would not become a reality until 1905, the Communist Party of the USA not until 1919.

Much earlier, in Pittsburgh during the great railroad strike of 1877, the legend that became Mother Jones was born. Mary demonstrated both her inspirational talent as a speaker as well as well-honed organisational skills.

She was part of the strikes that led to the Haymarket riot in Chicago in 1886 — the birth of May Day as a workers' celebration. In Birmingham, Alabama, she worked the textile mills of the Deep South, leading an important strike in 1894. She organised a famous march of children to protest about child labour.

Amazingly she found time to pen two important books — The New Right in 1899 and a two-volume Letter of Love and Labour in 1900 and 1901. Much of her efforts went on organising miners, first in the coalfields of West Virginia and Pennsylvania. She moved about, sometimes employed by the United Mine Workers. She lodged mostly with supporters and lived on food and a little money from grateful supporters.

In 1903, she split from the UMW when the right-wing national leadership refused to support a strike in the Colorado coalfields. Mother Jones stayed in the west for the next 10 years, organising copper miners in Idaho and Arizona.

In 1913, aged 83 she was sent to jail for 20 years for her part in a violent West Virginia strike. Huge public outrage demanded and won her freedom and Mother Jones headed for Colorado and the Ludlow strike.

After the Ludlow massacre she led the national crusade to get justice for the victims. That campaign forced Congress to investigate the massacre and the strike. Its report, published in 1915, opened the way to child labour laws and an eight-hour working day. Mary went on to help found the IWW and was a leading Wobbly organiser. She told her own story in the Autobiography of Mother Jones, published in 1925.

Mother Jones died in 1930. She had just celebrated her 100th birthday, although sources vary on her date of birth. She is buried in the Union Miners Cemetery in Mount Olive, Illinois, alongside miners murdered in the 1898 battle of Virden — working-class martyrs she always called "her boys." Mary Harris, Mother Jones, will never be forgotten.

ONE OF BRITAIN'S FUNNIEST WRITERS

SUE TOWNSEND

Obituary published April 24 2014.

It is 1969. The young single mum from Leicester was struggling at the bus stop with her three toddlers. Only one, aged five, is old enough to need a ticket and Mum is busy instructing him. "If the conductor asks how old you are, tell him you're four."

With just 11 pence in her purse, Mum has enough for her fare into town to join the long fight to collect her dole money, but not the boy's half fare. When the conductor arrives the lad looks at mum and asks: "Mum, am I four or five?"

That young Leicester mum, eldest of five sisters, left school at 15 destined for dead-end jobs in the town's hosiery factories, a petrol station or packing fish fingers for Birds Eye. She married at 18, had three children by the time she was 23. The marriage ended and she became a single parent struggling on benefits.

A dozen or so years on this mum will be a multi-millionaire and one of the widest-read authors and best-known playwrights in the world. But Sue Townsend, who died earlier this month aged 68, would never forget her humble origins nor stop campaigning for those who still struggle to find enough money for the bus fare.

Well-known for her many hugely funny books, this article celebrates the book she first published in 1989 exactly 25 years ago, Mr Bevan's Dream: Why Britain Needs Its Welfare State. It is non-fiction, but in a series of personal memories and anecdotes it make a passionate case for what was, and still is, going wrong as Tories, then as now, try to demolish the welfare state.

A quarter of a century ago, Townsend argued that the benefits system was unfair, inefficient and totally unprofessional — which is why millions of people do not claim the benefits to which they are legally entitled. She was still making that argument right up until her death.

Her better-known books, starting with The Diary Of Adrian Mole Aged 13¾, never hid her radical political views. We meet Bert the old communist, clearly based on an old comrade Townsend had known in Leicester. Bert sends the young Master Mole to the newsagent to get his newspaper. What else but the Morning Star?

When the boy asks Bert if the Morning Star is a newspaper, Townsend's politics comes echoing through in Bert's strident reply. "Are you backward? The Morning Star is the only newspaper worth reading. The others are owned by capitalist running dog lackeys."

Through Adrian's stumbling political awakening we learn all about Thatcher. "I'm not sure how I will vote. Sometimes I think Mrs Thatcher is a nice kind sort of woman. Then the next day I see her on television and she frightens me rigid. She has got eyes like a psychotic killer, but a voice like a gentle person. It is a bit confusing."

Other lessons, all woven with incredible humour, include war and peace, the horror of three million unemployed, as well as love, sex, sexuality, militant feminism, writing poetry and even holding your drink.

Adrian's ultimate lesson is about Labour politicians who betray their class. His beloved Pandora sells out to become an MP and one of "Blair's babes." Townsend's conscience makes sure the even Pandora's sell-out is not complete — she opposes the Iraq war.

The Adrian Mole books are full of these political messages and lessons, not always politically correct and often told through the actions of Adrian's mum Pauline, surely a barely disguised Townsend. Pauline goes to the Greenham women's peace camp. Adrian almost understands. "My mother has gone out with Mrs Singh, Mrs O'Leary and her women's group to have a picnic on Greenham Common."

Pauline reads Germaine Greer's The Female Eunuch and embraces feminism. "My mother has gone to a woman's workshop on assertiveness training," moans Adrian. "She came home and started bossing us around."

Townsend never hides her staunch republican principles. One Christmas, the old communist Bert tells Adrian's aunt that the royal family should be made to live on a council estate. That simple, but useful, idea became a whole book, The Queen And I, where a socialist government throws the royal family out of their palaces and the entire family move to a council estate.

The politics of the Gang of Four and the origins of the SDP and thus the Liberal Democrats gave the author a huge and entertaining new theme. Pandora's mother supports the Labour renegades in the SDP, her father loves Tony Benn. Violent arguments ensue and, when Adrian tries to help by posting a draft letter to the local Labour Party, chaos results.

Townsend always described herself as a passionate socialist, atheist and republican. Hating Tony Blair and New Labour, she enthusiastically supported the traditional views and the proud history of the Labour Party but said she had only voted Labour once. She told reporters she preferred to vote Communist, Socialist Worker or a for one of the minority left parties if she had the chance.

Townsend may have gone, and she will certainly be missed, but

Adrian Mole, Pandora Braithwaite and her many other characters and books will last forever. Most of her books are still in print — all, sadly, except Mr Bevan's Dream.

If you want some not-too-heavy political history of the last half a century as well as a really good laugh you could still do a lot worse than re-reading Sue Townsend.

THE CAGED BIRD THAT SANG

MAYA ANGELOU

Obituary published May 31 2014.

Maya Angelou, one of the foremost African-American writers, thinkers and activists of our time, has died in her North Carolina home aged 86. The respectable Establishment will mark her passing as a poet, writer and broadcaster but will be less keen to celebrate her record as an early and fierce civil rights champion.

Let us celebrate Dr Angelou — she always liked to be called by the title, probably because she never went to any university — as a true global renaissance woman. She was a celebrated poet, novelist, educator, dramatist, producer, actor, historian, film-maker, broadcaster as well as a leading political activist.

Above all this amazing woman was a courageous freedom fighter. Her greatest achievements were in the civil rights movement. She was close to two giants, both martyrs of that struggle, Malcolm X and Martin Luther King. Prior to his assassination, she and Malcolm X had plans to start a new movement to advance African-American rights.

Together they planned to found the Organisation of African-American Unity. They both intended to speak out on issues plaguing black people in the US to the United Nations. UN support, they believed, would cause the US real political embarrassment. In 1965 Malcolm was cut down by assassins. One dream ended.

For a number of years Angelou was a key leader of the Southern Christian Leadership Conference (SCLC). This organisation, founded by Martin Luther King, was an important body in the early struggle for civil rights in the US. The SCLC preached non-violence and organised protests, boycotts, marches and voter registration drives. Again King's political assassination hit hard but couldn't kill that dream.

Angelou offered her support to Cuban leader Fidel Castro, writing sympathetic articles when he was most hated by the US Establishment. This had the predictable result that she was branded a communist. Her response was truly poetic. "Wasn't no communist country that put my grandpappa in slavery," she declared. "Wasn't no communist lynched my poppa or raped my mamma."

Angelou was born into typical black poverty as Marguerite Ann Johnson in St Louis, Missouri, on April 4 1928. At just eight, she was raped by her mother's boyfriend.

When the rapist was beaten to death after Angelou testified against him, she cruelly blamed herself for his death. She thought her voice, her testimony, had killed him and she didn't speak again for almost six years.

In 1941 Angelou, aged just 13, won a scholarship to study dance and drama at San Francisco's Labour School. The school was close to the Communist Party (CPUSA) and was blacklisted as subversive by various state and federal bodies. The school gave the young Maya a good grounding, not just in music and dance but also in radical politics.

By the age of 14 lack of money forced her to drop out of school and take a job as a conductor on San Francisco's famous cable cars. She was the first African-American woman to hold such a job.

Later, and by now pregnant, she returned to finish high school, giving birth to her son Guy just a few weeks after graduation. As a young single mother, she supported herself and her child by working as a waitress and cook. In her late teens continuing poverty forced her into dancing in strip clubs and even into prostitution to augment the earnings from the career she was beginning to build as an actor, singer and dancer. Slowly recognition came and by 1954 she was touring 22 countries in Europe with a production of the opera Porgy and Bess.

She studied modern dance with Martha Graham, danced on TV and, in 1957, wrote and recorded her first album Miss Calypso.

In 1958 she moved to New York, where she acted in the historic off-Broadway production of Jean Genet's The Blacks and wrote and performed Cabaret for Freedom to raise funds and awareness for the civil rights movement.

James Baldwin and the Harlem Writers Guild helped her to develop her literary talents and her poems, novels, plays and — best known — her autobiographical books, which would make her famous and give her the voice and authority to speak out against injustice and inequality.

In the early '60s, Angelou, always an internationalist, supported the young anti-apartheid movement in South Africa. While working in Egypt and Ghana as a journalist and editor she met and became lifelong friends with Nelson Mandela. Mandela read aloud Angelou's poem Still I Rise at his 1994 presidential inauguration. In January this year after Mandela's death she published His Day Is Done, a poetic tribute to her great hero.

Angelou gained respect and fame for her writing. She produced seven books of semi-autobiography — most famously, I Know Why The Caged Bird Sings in 1969. It became an instant bestseller despite attempts to ban it from some reactionary quarters.

In 1993 president Bill Clinton asked Angelou to compose an original poem, titled On The Pulse Of The Morning, which she read at his inauguration.

In 1994 the National Association for the Advancement of Coloured People (NAACP) presented the writer and film-maker with the prestigious Spingarn Medal — the African-American Nobel Prize. It meant more to her than her Pulitzer Prize nomination, three Grammys and her many other awards.

In 2011 President Barack Obama awarded her with the Medal of Freedom, the US's highest civilian honour. However neither respectability nor getting older silenced her strident voice in support of valuable causes.

Last summer, Angelou spoke out about the acquittal of George Zimmerman, a white man who had shot and killed a black Florida teenager named Trayvon Martin. She told the media that "the jury verdict showed how far we still have to go as a nation."

She was a staunch advocate for marriage equality and was always ready to speak out against homophobia and religious bigotry. She told New York state Senator Shirley Huntley: "To love someone takes a lot of courage. So how much more when the love is of the same sex and the law forbids it." Her argument convinced Huntley to vote for the same-sex marriage bill before the legislature.

Just a few days before her death she made a strong case for action to recover the kidnapped Nigerian school girls. She tweeted: "Our future is threatened by the robbing of these young women's future. We must have our darlings back so that we can help them to heal."

The struggle for freedom and equality in the US, and indeed the rest of the world, has yet to be won. Recent advances by the forces of racism and reaction on this side of the Atlantic mean the world needs voices like Maya Angelou's more than ever.

Maya Angelou may be dead, but her writings, her poems, her powerful ideas and principles live on. The bird may have flown the cage, but we can all still hear her song.

SHE CAMPAIGNED FOR PEACE AND VOTES

MARGARET BONDFIELD

Published August 7 2014 in the Morning Star's special commemoration of World War I.

Suffragettes had fought hard for votes for women in the decades leading up to the first world war but, when war was actually declared, some leaders of the movement suspended the votes campaign to join in the jingoism of the war. Some leaders demanded that all suffragettes support the war effort. In return, the government released suffragettes from prison. Emmeline Pankhurst, who would later become a Tory parliamentary candidate, announced that all militants had to "fight for their country as they fought for the vote."

After receiving £2,000 from the government, Pankhurst organised a demonstration in London. The banners read: "We Demand the Right to Serve" and "For Men Must Fight and Women Must work." Christabel Pankhurst started a recruiting campaign among the men in the country. But not all suffragettes were taken in by the warmongering propaganda.

One, Margaret Bondfield, disagreed with this new policy. She helped to establish the Women's Peace Crusade to campaign for a negotiated peace.

Today Bondfield is not much remembered, except perhaps among the socialists, anti-war campaigners and feminists of my local market town Northampton where she was elected, in 1923, as one of the three first Labour women MPs.

I've always had a soft spot for Bondfield. In 1909 she wrote a book called Socialism for Shop Assistants. I have never been able to find a copy, but that title alone won my heart to her.

She learned her early radical political ideas from her parents and by the age of 14 Bondfield left home to become apprentice in a large draper's shop in Hove. She became friendly with one of her customers, Louisa Martindale, a strong advocate of women's rights. Through Bondfield she met progressive thinkers and discovered political books and periodicals.

In 1894 Bondfield went to live with her brother Frank in London where she found work in a shop. It didn't take long before she was elected to the Shop Assistants Union (SAU) district council. In 1896 the women's industrial council asked her to carry out an investigation into the pay and conditions of shop workers. The report was published in 1898, the same year she was appointed assistant secretary of the SAU.

By now, Bondfield was Britain's leading expert on shop workers and gave evidence to the select committee on shops (1902) and the select committee on the truck system (1907).

With Mary Macarthur, she established the first women's general union, the National Federation of Women Workers, in 1906. In 1908 Bondfield became secretary of the Women's Labour League. She was also active in the Women's Co-operative Guild, leading early campaigns for a minimum wage. The guild also fought for an improvement in child welfare and action to lower the infant mortality rate.

In 1910 the Liberal government asked Bondfield to serve as a member of its advisory committee on the Health Insurance Bill. She persuaded the government to introduce maternity benefits. In October 1916, Bondfield joined with George Lansbury and Macarthur to set up a new National Council for Adult Suffrage.

In 1929 prime minister Ramsay MacDonald appointed Bondfield as his new minister of labour. She was the first woman in history to gain a place in the British Cabinet. In the financial crisis of 1931, Bondfield supported the government policy of depriving some married women of unemployment benefit. It was not a popular move. She refused to join McDonald's national government and lost her seat in the 1931 general election.

On the anniversary of WWI the Establishment has been honouring warmongers and jingoistic generals. Let us instead honour Margaret Bondfield, who fought for peace and also achieved much more besides for the rights of women.

STAR WHO FOUGHT THE BLACKLIST

LAUREN BACALL

Obituary published August 16 2014.

Lauren Bacall, one of the last remaining icons of Hollywood's golden age, has died at her home in Manhattan. She was 89. Bacall became known for acting opposite her husband, Humphrey Bogart, in several 1940s classics including The Big Sleep, Key Largo and Dark Passage. She will best be remembered for two things. Teaching Bogart to whistle. "You know how to whistle, don't you, Steve? You just put your lips together and blow." It might have been her first film but was without doubt among the most memorable lines of all time.

She will also be remembered as one of those golden Hollywood female stars who despite, or perhaps because of, all the glitz and the glamour were such effective voices in campaigning for so many liberal, progressive and left-wing causes in US politics. The list is a long one, from Marilyn Monroe to Jane Fonda, and today from Susan Sarandon to Daryl Hannah.

Lauren Bacall was one of the earliest stars to put her career on the line by nailing her political colours to the mast. She campaigned for democrat Harry S Truman for president — she even posed sat on the top of a piano while Truman played.

In October 1947, Bacall persuaded her husband of two years Humphrey Bogart to join her in Washington to protest at the investigations of Hollywood and the entire US film industry by the red-baiting House Un-American Activities Committee (HUAC). Bogart was 45, Bacall just 20. In her first autobiography, By Myself, Bacall tells us that protest would be her "first grown-up exposure to a cause," and it would start a lifetime of political campaigning.

Bogart himself felt strongly about HUAC's McCarthite witch-hunts, but it was Bacall's passion that persuaded him to go with her to Washington. She was thrilled to be standing up for what she believed in. The protest didn't stop the disgraceful blacklisting, first of the Hollywood Ten and then of hundreds of talented writers, musicians, actors and other film-makers.

Bacall and Bogart helped form a Committee for the First Amendment. It called itself a non-political group of some of Hollywood's biggest stars, campaigning only for "honesty, fairness and the accepted rights of an American citizen."

The committee made a short film called Hollywood Fights Back and the deep female voiceover spells it out: "This is Lauren Bacall. Have you seen Crossfire yet? ... The American people have awarded it four stars. The Un-American Committee gave the man who made it a subpoena."

Bacall and Bogart's actions led to a media campaign accusing them of being communists — they weren't. A frightened Bogart even wrote a press article entitled I'm No Communist. Bacall was made of sterner stuff.

She told the Washington Daily News: "When I left the HUAC building I couldn't help but feel that every American who cares anything at all about preserving American ideals should witness part of this investigation. It starts with Hollywood, but I'm sorry to say I don't think it will end with us."

Her experience in that early political campaign began a life for her as an outspoken champion of so many causes. Perhaps her proudest moment was her enthusiastic support of the Nuclear Freeze Movement in the 1980s. She spoke at meetings and rallies all over the country helping to make this a key chapter in the history of US anti-war and anti-nuclear weapons movements.

Over her long life and career she used her name and fame to help and support many Democratic Party leaders including Adlai Stevenson, Robert Kennedy, Bill Clinton, Barack Obama and much more recently Hillary Clinton.

Bacall was born Betty Joan Perske on September 16 1924 in The Bronx, New York. Her Jewish background brought its share of anti-semitism and in life she learned to hate all kind of racism and intolerance. Much later she would discover that Shimon Peres who became the prime minister of Israel was a family relative. Although she did visit him in Tel Aviv on one occasion there is no evidence that she offered him any political support.

After graduating from high school, she entered the American Academy of Dramatic Arts and worked as a model, landing on the cover of Harper's Bazaar. That is where the wife of director Howard Hawks first saw her and suggested her husband give her a screen test. Hawks changed her name from Betty to Lauren. The last name Bacall was the maiden name of her mother.

In 1944 Hawks cast Bacall in the role of Marie "Slim" Browning in the film To Have And Have Not based on a story by Ernest Hemingway. The choice for the male star was between Cary Grant and Humphrey Bogart. Lauren rather fancied Grant. Bogart, of course, got the part and by the spring of 1945 they were married. Bacall had two children with Bogart. He died from oesophageal cancer in 1957.

A year later, she became engaged to Frank Sinatra, but he broke off the match. "He behaved like a complete shit," Bacall said later. She coined the term "The Rat Pack" to describe Bogart, Sinatra and their friends.

From 1961 to 1969, she was married to actor Jason Robards, with whom she had another son, Sam.

When it seemed Hollywood had tired of Lauren Bacall she moved from the silver screen to live theatre and continued to win both awards and public acclaim. There was a brief but successful return to making movies and more recently her career continued with TV and animated voiceovers. The honours and awards kept coming as her career wound down.

So let's sum up and leave the last word to the star herself. In 2005 Bacall told TV's Larry King that she was "anti-Republican and a liberal. The L-word. Being a liberal is the best thing on Earth you can be. You are welcoming to everyone when you're a liberal. You do not have a small mind."

DOYEN OF WORKING CLASS THEATRE

JOAN LITTLEWOOD

Published October 4 2014 the centenary of the birth of the founding mother of working-class theatre in Britain.

Born 100 years ago this weekend, Joan Littlewood changed the face of British theatre forever. Her great loves — agitprop, political and community theatre, speaking out in working-class language — have passed into mainstream culture both on stage and screen. Littlewood, who died in 2002 aged 87, devoted her whole life to community theatre.

Late in life she said: "I really do believe in the community, I really do believe in the genius in every person." The Theatre Royal at Stratford, east London, remains a lasting tribute to her. This year her production of Oh What a Lovely War! has been celebrated and has refocused interest on her, but there is much more to salute and pay tribute to in this, her centenary year.

Joan Maud Littlewood was born in Stockwell, south London, to an unmarried mother who disapproved of books. However her grandmother, who did most of the childcare, was known as a fine teller of — often bawdy — jokes and stories. As soon as she could read Littlewood herself adopted the dangerous hobby of reading library books by candlelight under the bedclothes out of mother's sight.

Young Littlewood's first contact with the world of the stage was an approach by one of Stan Laurel's scouts. She played a few small comedy parts in local shows.

Her first brush with politics was aged 12 in the general strike. She questioned her grandfather on why the strike had been defeated after just 10 days. "What do you want, a communist red revolution?" grandpa asked the young Littlewood. She didn't hesitate. "Yes," she answered. It would be her political credo for life.

She won a scholarship to a convent school, fortuitously just a short walk from the Old Vic. Theatre visits rather than formal schooling set her course for life and she applied for and won the only London scholarship to the then rather posh and middle-class Royal Academy of Dramatic Art. Despite winning awards and acting with George Bernard Shaw, the atmosphere at Rada and their views on what theatre should be about, didn't suit Littlewood and after just a year she decided to head for the US. She started out by walking to Liverpool.

She got 130 miles on foot to Burton-on-Trent before collapsing. She begged or borrowed the fare to Manchester, to meet an ex-Rada teacher and communist Archie Harding, whose left-wing views had seen him exiled to Manchester by the BBC. In Manchester she found, and loved, a culture of small, leftist agitprop groups dedicated to taking drama to working people.

In this new and exciting world she met fellow young communist Jimmie Miller. Later he would become folk singer Ewan MacColl. They married and together they founded the Theatre of Action in 1934. Littlewood and MacColl subsidised their communist work by acting and reading for the BBC but all their energy went into what by 1936 had become Theatre Union.

Theatre Union productions were influenced by Brecht, Stanislavsky, Meyerhold and Expressionist movement pioneer Rudolf Laban. The inspiration Littlewood herself returned to most often was the commedia dell'arte — travelling troupes of radical players in 16th-century Italy.

During the war Littlewood and MacColl's work was often splendidly reviewed but always refused official funding. The couple were blacklisted by the BBC and by forces entertainment group ENSA as subversives. MI5 kept detailed files on them both. Despite this, at the end of the war, such was Littlewood's artistic reputation the BBC asked for her help with features and drama.

Instead, in 1945, she and her company, now renamed Theatre Workshop, hired a lorry and took to the road. Two teenage communists, Howard Goorney and Gerry Raffles, joined the tour. Both would become lifelong parts of her company and life. Goorney as a principal actor, Raffles the indispensable backstage organiser.

Raffles soon replaced MacColl in Littlewood's affections despite being her junior by nine years. Their relationship would last more than 30 years. Raffles hitchhiked and slept rough as he searched working-class communities for venues where the group could perform. Although audiences loved the shows, money and bookings were hard to find.

In 1953, Littlewood and Raffles found a disused and scruffy theatre to rent in east London. MacColl left to concentrate on folk singing and recording.

The Theatre Royal, Angel Lane, Stratford, smelled strongly of cat's pee but the rent was just £20 a week. They moved in, got rid of that smell, and again changed the face of British theatre forever.

Outstanding performances included Harry H Corbett — later TV's Harold Steptoe and the only communist to be linked romantically to Princess Margaret — in an award-winning Richard II. The 1955 production of the Czech play Good Soldier Schweik transferred to the West End. Many other productions too moved from Stratford to successful West End runs.

Among them were Shelagh Delaney's A Taste of Honey, Brendan Behan's The Hostage, Lionel Bart's Fings Ain't Wot They Used T'Be, Wolf Mankowitz's Make Me An Offer and Stephen Lewis's Sparrers Can't Sing. Many of these shows were uproarious working-class comedies but with a serious message. All were a reaction to the stultified, overwhelmingly middle-class West End theatre. In 1956 Behan's anti-capital punishment prison drama The Quare Fellow drew full houses.

Many what are now well known names started under Littlewood's tutelage. These included Yootha Joyce, Glynn Edwards, Richard Harris, Brian Murphy, Nigel Hawthorne and Barbara Windsor. Not all impressed Littlewood. She told the young Michael Caine after only one production: "Piss off to Shaftesbury Avenue. You will only ever be a star."

Some West End successes eventually gave her and Raffles enough money to purchase the theatre but for Littlewood the spark had dimmed. Exhausted and deflated, she travelled alone to Nigeria to work on a film project that never happened.

Back in London she launched her plan for a Fun Palace — a Thames-side entertainment promenade, with music, lectures, plays and restaurants. It was as if she had foreseen the O2 Dome, but it never happened for her.

She returned to Stratford in 1975 for her last, and perhaps best-known, success with Oh, What A Lovely War!, a work of genius in which a lifetime's creativity and politics came together.

A revival of that show to celebrate the centenary of the start of World War I has put Littlewood back in the limelight. Centre-stage is exactly where she deserves to be a century after her birth.

FEMALE NOBEL PRIZE WINNERS ARE RARE INDEED

MALALA YOUSAFZAI AND DOROTHY HODGKIN

Published October 14 2014 when Malala Yousafzai became only the 46th woman to win the Nobel Prize. This is the story of an earlier winner part of the Red Science movement.

Malala Yousafzai, the 17-year-old Pakistani female education activist, shot and wounded but never silenced by the Taliban, became the youngest ever Nobel Peace Prize recipient on October 10 2014.

Few women have ever won a Nobel Prize. Of the 867 awards distributed since 1901, just 46 have gone to women. I was researching and writing the story of another female Nobel laureate from exactly 50 years ago when I read of Malala's great news in the Morning Star.

In the autumn of 1964 Dorothy Crowfoot Hodgkin, a British chemist, became one of only four women who had ever won the Nobel Prize for chemistry. Her prize was awarded for her pioneering work in protein crystallography. The prize rewarded her more than 30 years of pioneering biochemical research that helped unravel the structures of proteins, including insulin and, among many other things, advanced the control of diabetes.

Dorothy Hodgkin was born Dorothy Mary Crowfoot in 1910. She studied chemistry at Somerville College, Oxford, but moved to Cambridge University in 1932 to work on the development of X-ray crystallography with famous communist scientist JD Bernal. The couple had a close personal and political relationship.

Over the next four years Hodgkin and Bernal produced a dozen joint crystallographic papers. They also shared a Marxist view of the world. The two were part of what at the time was often known as Red Science.

Novelist and chemist CP Snow told communist historian Eric Hobsbawm that if they took a poll of a couple of hundred of the brightest young British scientists in the mid 1930s, they would have found around 15 Communist Party members, a good 50 more on the left and 100 more proud of their leftist views.

In 1939 Bernal wrote his book The Social Function of Science. The work focuses on the way resources were allocated to various parts of science and technology. At the heart of Bernal's book — indeed his whole political thinking, and Hodgkin's too — is a call to organise this great human power of science to serve the many, not the few.

In 1937, Dorothy married Thomas Lionel Hodgkin although her close relationship with Bernal would continue on and off for many years. Her published letters show that neither she, nor her husband, nor Bernal had much time for conventional relationships.

Her new husband would become an Oxford lecturer, a member of the Communist Party and an advisor to Kwame Nkrumah, who took the Gold Coast, later Ghana, to independence from British rule. Hodgkin and her husband would spend much time with Nkrumah, often described as the Lenin of Africa, in Ghana.

In the 1950s her and her husband's communist politics would lead to her being banned from entering the US. This severely limited international research with US scientists. She was allowed just a few transatlantic visits by special permission from the CIA.

Around this time she and her old friend and mentor Bernal had key roles in the World Peace Council. This too brought them to the attention of the secret services on both sides of the Atlantic. The pair worked together when the British Peace Committee attempted to host a world peace congress in Sheffield. British government obstructions caused a number of delegates to be stranded in London.

One was Pablo Picasso. At a gathering the artist drew a large dove of peace on Bernal's sitting room wall. Today the drawing can be seen at London's Wellcome Collection.

In April 1953 Hodgkin travelled from Oxford to Cambridge to see the model of the double helix structure of DNA. Credit for the model and another Nobel Prize went to Francis Crick and James Watson, but much of the research had been carried out by another female chemist, and a close colleague of Hodgkin, Rosalind Franklin.

The two had discussed Franklin's early X-ray photographs of the double helix a decade before Crick and Watson got their DNA Nobel Prize. Franklin has never been given the credit she deserves for her work on DNA. Many think she should have been a third Nobel nomination along with Crick and Watson.

Hodgkin published as Dorothy Crowfoot until 1949, when she was persuaded to use her married name. Hodgkin was always just as concerned about political and world issues as her scientific research. She was president of the Pugwash Conferences on Science and World Affairs from 1976 to 1988.

Pugwash is an international organisation that brings together scientists, scholars and public figures to work toward reducing the danger of armed conflict and to seek solutions to global security threats. It was founded in Pugwash, Nova Scotia, in 1957 by Joseph Rotblat and Bertrand Russell. Rotblat and the Pugwash Conference jointly won the Nobel Peace Prize in 1995 for their efforts on nuclear disarmament.

Sadly Hodgkin's reputation took a knock when she was swept into a scientific fraud involving Elena Ceausescu, the wife of the president of communist Romania. Hodgkin wrote the foreword to the English edition of a scientific paper supposedly written by Ceausescu. Hodgkin quoted Ceausescu's "outstanding achievements" and "impressive" career. We now know that Ceausescu never finished secondary school, never attended university, that her scientific credentials and work were a complete fraud.

All the research published under her name throughout her life was written by a team of uncredited scientists. The incident cast a dark shadow over Hodgkin's reputation as well as on science from the communist world.

As well as her Nobel Prize, Hodgkin received many other honours. Even the US forgave her communist politics. In 1958, she was elected a foreign honorary member of the American Academy of Arts and Sciences. She was only the second woman to receive the Order of Merit in 1965 — the first was Florence Nightingale. Hodgkin was awarded the Soviet Union's Lenin Peace Prize in 1987. She died in 1994.

Hodgkin had some interesting, if unexpected, admirers. In the 1940s, one of her chemistry students was Margaret Roberts, who would become prime minister Maggie Thatcher. Thatcher hung a portrait of Hodgkin in 10 Downing Street — probably the only communist portrait ever to grace those walls.

Malala Yousafzai has shown just how impressive a woman needs to be to win a Nobel Prize.

Fifty years ago Dorothy Hodgkin did exactly the same and she remains the only British woman to have ever won one of the science Nobel Prizes. Let's salute these two women, half a century apart but who both demonstrate that, as a man called Mao Zedong once said, "women really do hold up half the sky" whatever the Nobel Prize judging panel may usually think.

BEAUTIFUL MIND
HEDY LAMARR

Published November 18 2014 to mark the centenary of the birth of Hedy Lamarr — not just once known as the most beautiful woman in the world but also as an anti-nazi and a great scientist.

My recent obituary of Lauren Bacall (p55) surprised a good few readers. Most knew her as a film star but the other side of her life as a champion of progressive causes was obviously far less well known. One or two of my fellow movie buffs suggested I tell the even less known story of Hedy Lamarr, not just because she was generally agreed to be the most beautiful woman in the world in her time, but as an anti-nazi, U-boat saboteur and inventor, sort of, of today's mobile phones and wi-fi.

Hedwig Kiesler was born, exactly a century ago, into a boring bourgeois family in Vienna. The first world war came late to the city but when it did it would end the once mighty Austro-Hungarian empire forever. Her father, a banker, had no preconceived ideas about what young girls should be interested in.

On long walks he explained to his bright and curious little girl the workings of all kinds of new and exciting inventions, steam-powered printing presses, electric tramcars, paddle-steamers on the Danube and the newest sensation, the Bioscope shows — moving pictures on the silver screen. The young Hedwig had little problem understanding how these modern marvels worked. She could, it seemed, quickly grasp sophisticated technical concepts.

Rather than pursue a technical career, though, it was the silver screen that attracted her. She became an actor. Still in her teens, she starred in the amazing 1933 film Ekstase (Ecstasy). The film was made in three language versions — Czech, German and French. It chalked up several firsts in legitimate cinema — first nude scenes, first female orgasm, first sexual intercourse on screen.

The Czech romantic drama is about a young woman, played by Kiesler, who marries a wealthy but much older man. Leaving her brief loveless marriage, she takes up with a virile young engineer who becomes her lover. The film was hugely controversial and very successful, mostly because of scenes in which Lamarr swims and runs through the countryside naked.

It made her an overnight star and like many a young star she married young and unwisely. Fritz Mandl was a multi-millionaire arms manufacturer and an enthusiastic fascist. The Kieslers were a Jewish family but Hedy's mother became a very public Roman Catholic. It certainly fooled the anti-semitic Mandl.

Once married he tried to stop his young bride making any more films, even buying and destroying all the copies of Ekstase he could find. It didn't take much of this behaviour, nor what Hedy saw happening to her own home country and neighbouring Germany, to make her feel trapped. She came up with a cunning escape plan.

Mandl would invite his cronies — scientists, weapon inventors, senior political figures and fascists — to dinner. Both Hitler and Mussolini were dinner guests. At the table would be his attractive and clearly dumb young wife. She would flutter her eyelashes, act simple and stash away all kinds of useful classified intelligence. She reckoned it would buy her a new life somewhere in the future.

It worked. She threatened to expose her husband's stupidity and he had no alternative but to let her go. She dressed herself in all the many jewels her husband had bought her and headed first to Paris and then across the Atlantic. Keisler's slightly lurid film reputation landed a Hollywood movie deal. She changed her name and headed for California.

Now, although all over the billboards as Hedy Lamarr, she never lost her early interest in all things technical. Even between shoots at the studio or on location she experimented with all kinds of inventions. Among her many creations were a sweet Oxo-type cube to turn plain water into cola and a non-surgical skin-tautening technique —

ironically much later in her career she would have much disastrous cosmetic surgery.

It was in WWII together with a musician neighbour named George Antheil that she had the idea that would change the way we all live today. German U-boats had been harassing transatlantic convoys. They had killed many civilians including large groups of children. The U-boat captains could block the radio guidance systems of allied torpedoes.

Hedy knew all about these systems and blocking them — she had often heard them discussed over the dinner table back in Vienna. She knew that radio-controlled torpedoes could easily be jammed by broadcasting interference at the frequency of the control signal, causing the torpedo to go off course. She concluded that using frequency-hopping — jumping from one frequency to another — would prevent jamming and let the torpedo hit its U-boat target. But how could frequent and unpredictable channel hopping be arranged?

Antheil, her avant-garde composer neighbour, provided the answer from a somewhat unexpected source. He had experimented with automated control of musical instruments, including his music for futurist painter Fernand Leger's 1924 abstract film Ballet Mecanique. This score involved multiple player-pianos playing simultaneously. Antheil and Lamarr adapted a pierced paper piano roll to unpredictably change the signal sent between a ship and its torpedo to any of 88 frequencies.

Why 88? There are 88 keys on a piano. Both ship and torpedo would have the same code so it would be impossible for the U-boat to scan and jam all 88 frequencies. Sadly the US navy was slow to adopt the idea, no doubt because it came from a movie star and a nutty composer. Indeed when Lamarr applied to join the National Inventors Council she was told she could better help the war effort by using her celebrity status and her looks to sell war bonds.

Today Lamarr and Anthel's spread-spectrum communication technology is the foundation for Bluetooth and many wifi, cordless and wireless telephones. In 1997 their work was finally recognised. They

were honoured with special awards for their "trailblazing development of a technology that has become a key component of wireless
data systems."

Not perhaps what you might expect from someone who was just the
"most beautiful woman in the world."

CHAMPION OF
BRITAIN'S HERITAGE

SONIA ROLT

Obituary published November 29 2014.

Sonia Rolt, who has died aged 95, made a massive contribution
to the preservation and appreciation of Britain's industrial and
cultural heritage. Perhaps best known as the grande dame of
Britain's waterways, she didn't just campaign for the preservation of
canals but also fought and agitated for better wages and conditions for
those families who worked the boats. The trading narrow boats were
her first love but she also involved herself in the preservation of steam
railways, historic ships and old buildings.

She was born Sonia South in New York to British parents and or-
phaned when young. After a convent education she trained in acting
at the London Theatre Studio. She lived with two other rather posh
young ladies in London's Beauchamp Place, next door to Harrods.

The second world war's directed labour scheme sent this unlikely
trio to the elegant Hoover factory at Perivale where they were trained
to solder wiring in Lancaster bombers. At this time the Communist
Party was busy organising female labour in the engineering factories
of west London. Perhaps because of Sonia's reputation as a left-wing

firebrand she was interviewed by Special Branch about communist influence in the Hoover factory.

When Sonia and her comrades saw a Ministry of Transport advertisement seeking women to work boats on the Grand Union Canal they volunteered, attracted by the outdoor life and the fact that they would be paid by how much they carried, and under nobody's orders.

The Ministry of Labour, already somewhat suspicious of Sonia, at first said No. She was threatened with imprisonment for what they said was an unpatriotic attempt to change jobs. In the end a Ministry of Labour psychiatrist said she and her flatmates could go. They were perhaps glad to see her away from the politics of the factory floor.

Sonia with her two flatmates was sent for brief training on the water. It was the first canal any of them had ever seen. They became Idle Women, the rather unkind joke on the IW badges they wore — the IW really stood for Inland Waterways. They certainly weren't idle. The trio worked long hours and lived on a pair of cramped and unhygienic narrow-boats carrying 50 tons of metal from London to Birmingham. They carried coal from the Midlands collieries on the return journey.

The work was hard, conditions harsh and cramped but the three women loved the life and Sonia in particular fell in love with the canal boat folk, their way of life and the beauty in the locks, bridges and buildings of the waterways. It was her first introduction to the wonders of Britain's industrial landscape.

It didn't take long for these three young women to attract the attentions of the young male boaters working with their parents on the canals. One such was a handsome young boatman with amazing blonde curls called George Smith. Smith was illiterate, perhaps because he had lived all his life on the cut. To Sonia he seemed to know everything about waterways. The unlikely couple fell in love.

Sonia and George were married in 1945, and together they worked a pair of boats. They also encouraged canal workers to join the union and fought for better conditions on the canal ways.

The couple also campaigned for Labour in the July 1945 election that brought an Attlee landslide victory. A contemporary photograph shows her chalking election slogans on her boat Phobus.

They made a handsome couple, so handsome that they featured in some of the early documentary films made to celebrate canal transport in the immediate post-war pre-nationalisation period. It was at a screening of one of these films in Birmingham she first met Tom Rolt. Rolt had published his book Narrow Boat in 1944. It would be the most important foundation stone for what would become the canal preservation movement.

The book was an account of his life and cruising with his first wife, Angela, aboard their converted narrow boat Cressy. Rolt became one of the leading campaigners for canals, co-founding the Inland Waterways Association (IWA) in 1946. Sonia and Rolt soon started campaigning together. He thought her a scary left-wing blue-stocking. She thought him soft, having a bath aboard his boat Cressy. As time went on they got closer and closer both as activists and then as a couple.

Sonia became an effective spokeswoman to the government and trade unions. She and Rolt campaigned for better working conditions, especially after the canals were nationalised in 1947.

In 1951, the IWA split. Rolt was expelled. His wife Angela had left to join Billy Smart's circus as its first ever female ringmaster. Sonia and Smith drifted apart although she stayed friends with him all her life. Smith died in 2012 and Sonia dedicated her 1997 book, A Canal People: The Photographs of Robert Longden, to him and his second wife.

In 1952, now both divorced, Sonia and Rolt married. Tom was by then chair of the Talyllyn railway in mid-Wales. He had been behind the idea of saving this narrow-gauge steam railway, which became the first preserved railway in the world.

The Rolts moved to run the railway together. He became the mechanic and engineer, while Sonia did everything else. They moved into his family home at Stanley Pontlarge, near Cheltenham. The 14th-century house had no roof, paraffin lamps and open fires.

Sonia took advice from the Society for the Protection of Ancient Buildings and was soon a member of its committee. Later she would advise on the restoration of HMS Warrior and Isambard Kingdom Brunel's steamship Great Britain.

The founder of the conservation charity the Landmark Trust, John Smith, asked her to help furnish rescued buildings. She did and also helped the National Trust in the same way. Sonia got an OBE in 2011 for services to heritage and industrial archaeology.

However, if you seek a better more tangible honour, take a walk along your nearest canal towpath or a ride on a preserved steam railway. They wouldn't exist without the efforts of pioneers like Sonia Rolt.

NOT JUST UNSEEN BUT UNHEARD TOO

ETHEL SMYTH

Published March 8 2015 for International Women's Day.

This year Dame Ethel Smyth finally became Radio 3's Composer of the Week in the run-up to the celebration of International Women's Day. The recognition has been a long time coming. But that is only to be expected if, like Smyth, you don't just write six fine operas and an array of chamber, orchestral and vocal works but also upset the Establishment by throwing stones through the window of the colonial secretary.

It didn't stop with breaking windows. She also stormed 10 Downing Street itself to hammer out the her suffragette anthem the March of Women on prime minister Herbert Asquith's piano while the Cabinet was still in session. These militant activities saw her, with 200 sister suffragettes sentenced to two months in Holloway Prison. Sir Thomas Beecham went to visit her in jail and afterwards told this story.

"I arrived in the main courtyard of the prison to find the noble company of martyrs marching round it and singing lustily their war-chant while the composer, beaming approbation from an overlooking upper window, beat time in almost Bacchic frenzy with a toothbrush."

Smyth led a fascinating and unconventional life. She overcame opposition from her army father in order to enrol at the Leipzig Conservatorium in 1877 where she won respect from Johannes Brahms, Clara Schumann, Edvard Grieg and Pyotr Tchaikovsky. Tchaikovsky, rather sexist and patronisingly, said of her: "Miss Smyth is one of the few women composers whom one can seriously consider to be achieving something valuable in the field of musical creation." Back in England in the late 1880s, her music attracted much attention from influential figures including Thomas Beecham, Adrian Boult, Henry Wood and George Bernard Shaw praising her work.

Smyth became a leading and militant suffragette in the early 1910s. She met, and became enchanted by, Emmeline Pankhurst, and they eventually became lovers. Openly bisexual, usually dressed in men's tweeds and deerstalker cap, Smyth flaunted convention by having affairs, not just with Pankhurst but with Virginia Woolf, married opera librettist Henry B Brewster and a number of other notable men and women of the time. She shared a Surrey cottage with three famous sisters Millicent Garrett Fawcett, Elizabeth Garrett Anderson and Agnes Garrett.

She still remains the only female composer to have had an opera performed at the New York Met. Her most famous opera, The Wreckers, has been compared with Benjamin Britten's Peter Grimes but it is rarely performed. The last recording was made over 20 years ago.

Smyth wrote some of her best music for the Votes for Women cause. Her March of the Women came to be adopted as the suffragette anthem. It still has the power to inspire today.

Later in life increasing deafness curtailed her composing and she turned to writing a series of revealing autobiographies. In 1939, when war had shut down BBC music and concerts, Smyth was still showing her political sympathies. In a letter to the Daily Telegraph she suggested that a programme of free concerts broadcast from provinces "would lift up the hearts of many ... and ease the situation of a class of unemployed the thought of whom gives one perpetual heartache."

In 1937 she gave an interview to the BBC describing her suffragette stone-throwing. You can still hear it online.

THE SUFFRAGETTE IN THE AIRSHIP

MURIEL MATTERS

*Published February 16 2015 the actual day of a
remarkable flight 106 years before.*

During the struggle to win votes for women in Britain in the
first couple of decades of the 20th century, suffragettes became masters of the art of gaining media attention with elab-
orate and imaginative actions. One of the most audacious examples of
this was an airship flown over London on this day in 1909 by Muriel
Matters. Matters was a master in imaginative publicity for her cause.

She was born in Australia, coming to Britain in 1905, aged 28. She
was a professional pianist, elocutionist and actress before coming to
England, where she also became a talented journalist.

Matters became involved with the suffragette movement and was
a leading member of the Women's Freedom League (WFL), a split
from the better known Women's Social and Political Union (WSPU).
The WFL had been established in 1907 when Matters and some other
leading members of the WSPU began to question the leadership of
Emmeline and Christabel Pankhurst.

The Pankhursts became unpopular with some suffragettes by making decisions without consulting members and they challenged those
who did not accept their leadership to leave the WSPU and to form an
organisation of their own. Seventy leading members left to form the
WFL. Like the WSPU, the WFL was a militant organisation that was
willing the break the law.

Members of the WFL however were generally non-violent and disagreed with the WSPU campaign of vandalism and arson against private and commercial property. Despite this over 100 WFL members
were still sent to prison. The WFL soon had over 4,000 members and
it had its own newspaper, The Vote.

Matters was in charge of another publicity first — a horse-drawn recruiting caravan that toured the country. Most WFL members were pacifists and during World War I they refused to become involved in the British army's recruitment drive or to call off the votes for women campaign while the war was on. WFL members supported the Women's Peace Crusade for a negotiated peace.

Matters first came to prominence by chaining herself to a grille in the Ladies' Gallery of the House of Commons. While the authorities sent for a blacksmith to cut her free she made a speech. The 1908 stunt was almost certainly the first speech ever made by a woman in the House of Commons.

When she learned that King Edward VII was to lead a public procession to officially open Parliament on February 16 1909 she knew this was an occasion not to be missed. What was needed was something that would seize the headlines for the female emancipation.

Matters was not only a suffragette, she was also a great socialist and counted among her circle of left-wing friends people such as Sylvia Pankhurst, George Bernard Shaw and the Russian anarchist Peter Kropotkin.

Another socialist friend and a keen supporter of the suffragette cause was Henry Spencer. It was not, however, Spencer's politics that caught her attention. It was his most unusual hobby. Spencer had built his own airship and flew the 80-foot hydrogen-filled dirigible from a small field near the Welsh Harp Lake in Hendon, north of London. The lake is still there, beside the North Circular road.

Matters explained her plan to the bold aeronaut. They would load his airship, suitably painted with suffrage slogans, with a hundredweight of pamphlets and rain them down over the king's procession.

I'll let Matters take up the story as she did in a 1939 interview with the BBC. "That morning I went to Hendon and met Mr Henry Spencer who had his airship all ready near the Welsh Harp. It was quite a little airship, 88 feet long, and written in large letters on the gas bag were three words: Votes for women.

"Below this was suspended an extremely fragile rigging carrying the engine and a basket, like those used for balloons. We loaded up about a hundredweight of leaflets, then I climbed into the basket. Mr Spencer joined me and we rose into the air."

The airship, despite the weight of two people and all that propaganda, climbed to an altitude of 3,500 feet before levelling off. "It was very cold," Matters said, "but I got some exercise throwing the leaflets overboard."

She went on to describe how Spencer would climb out of the basket and clamber like a spider across the framework to make adjustments to the engine. "Suddenly I realised that if he fell off, I hadn't the first idea how to manoeuvre the airship." she said. "Not that I was terribly bothered about that. I was too busy making a trail of leaflets across London."

With the airship emblazoned with "Votes for Women" on one side and "Women's Freedom League" on the other she scattered 56lb of handbills onto the streets and houses below. Edith How-Martyn and Elsie Craig, two leading members of the Women's Freedom League, followed the airship in a car. Unfortunately, the elements conspired against the suffragette cause. The airship's feeble motor was not enough to overcome the strong winds that blew it off course.

The airship never made it to the Palace of Westminster but drifted across London, passing over Wormwood Scrubs, Kensington, Tooting and eventually crash-landing — after a trip lasting an hour-and-a-half — in the upper branches of a tree in Coulsdon, Surrey.

Despite failing to fly over the king and his procession, Matters considered the aerial adventure a great success. "The flight achieved all we wanted," she said. "It got our movement a great deal of publicity, as you can imagine. In those days, the sight of an airship was enough to make people run for miles." Certainly the unique flight made headlines all across Britain and the world.

After her aerial adventure, Matters continued with her political life as an active suffragette lecturing all over the world. She was an active campaigner against the first world war and stood as the Labour Party candidate for Hastings in the general election of 1924.

She went on to study in Barcelona under Maria Montessori, the radical Italian educationalist, returning to work at Sylvia Pankhurst's school in Bow, east London. Matters, the Suffragette in the airship, died in 1969 aged 92.

You can hear Muriel Matters telling her own story in her 1939 BBC radio interview www.bbc.co.uk/archive/suffragettes/8315.shtml.

THE LAST WOMAN HANGED IN BRITAIN
RUTH ELLIS

Published April 4 2015. An Easter Sunday 1955 shooting outside a pub in Hampstead started a controversy that is still being argued about 60 years later.

This Easter, just like every Easter, Londoners and visitors to the capital will take themselves to Hampstead Heath for a quick thrill on the fun fair or simply a peaceful stroll. After the heath what could be more natural than an evening drink in one of Hampstead's popular pubs. One of the nearest is the Magdala in South Hill Park just off the heath. This Easter the Magdala is closed, promising to reopen any day now.

By contrast 60 years ago, on Easter Sunday evening, the bar of the Magdala was busy with the usual mixture of locals and thirsty walkers back from the heath. Chief subject of bar-room gossip was the still fresh scandal involving a local murder. Ms Styllou Christofi, who had lived a few houses from the pub, had been hanged for the murder of her daughter-in-law at her home just a few months before. Christofi had been the last woman hanged in England but events that evening outside this Hampstead pub would rewrite those particular pages of legal and political history for ever.

Drinking in the pub was David Blakely, an up-and-coming racing driver who had just had a try-out for the year's Le Mans 24-hour race, and his friend Clive Gunnell. At about 10.30pm a taxi pulled up in Tanza Road a quarter of a mile from the pub. A young woman got out. Ruth Ellis was looking for her boyfriend. She thought he would be at the flat of his friends Anthony and Carole Findlater but as she arrived she saw his car drive away.

Ellis guessed where he might be and these thoughts were confirmed after a short walk to the Magdala pub. Parked outside was Blakely's car. As Blakely and Gunnell emerged from the pub, she stepped out of a newsagent's doorway and said: "Hello, David." He ignored her.

As Blakely fumbled for his car keys, Ellis took a revolver from her handbag and fired five shots. The first shot missed and Blakely sought shelter behind his car. Ellis's second shot felled him and she then stood over him and fired three more bullets at point-blank range.

The gun then seems to have jammed before Ellis finally got off her sixth and final shot. This one ricocheted off the road and hit the thumb of passerby Gladys Yule. Ellis, in a state of shock, asked Blakely's friend Gunnell: "Will you call the police, Clive?"

Off-duty policeman Alan Thompson took the still-smoking gun from her and put it in his coat pocket as he made the arrest. She told Thompson: "I am guilty, I'm a little confused," and at Hampstead police station she made a detailed confession and was charged with murder.

Today, investigators would have probed deeper. Where did she get the gun? Had her other lover Desmond Cussens provided the weapon and encouraged the shooting out of jealousy? Was Ellis suffering from post-miscarriage depression? Had Blakely's violent abuse provoked the killing?

Today the answers to these and other questions might result, depending on the judge, in a much more humane outcome — help and support rather than the noose. Sadly our jails still house female victims of domestic abuse who had the temerity to fight back.

But these were harsher, simpler times. Sixty years ago it didn't take long for the legal process to bring Ellis to trial, find her guilty and pronounce the death penalty. Thousands protested at the sentence but home secretary Major Lloyd George, a Liberal and Conservative MP (and you thought Cameron and Clegg invented that nonsense), refused to reprieve Ellis. Like all his Cabinet, he was a keen supporter of hanging.

Just before 9am on Wednesday July 13 1955 the official hangman Albert Pierrepoint walked Ellis from her cell to the gallows in Holloway Prison. They waited one minute, expecting a reprieve but it never came. Ellis went to her death. She was just 28.

Ellis would be the last woman to be hanged in Britain and her case, as much as any other, would lead to the huge public outcry that would finally abolish capital punishment a decade later. Sadly it took many tragic, wasted judicial deaths and a good few miscarriages of justice, including Ellis's, to persuade the Establishment to finally see sense.

Ruth Neilson was born in Rhyl in October 1926. She spent her childhood in Basingstoke. In 1941, at the height of the Blitz, her family moved to London. At 17 Neilson became pregnant. The father was a married Canadian soldier who soon disappeared. She gave birth to a son, Andy.

Various factory and clerical jobs were soon replaced by better money as a nightclub hostess, nude model and occasional prostitute. She worked at the Court Club in Mayfair where she became close friends with Diana Dors. Club manager Morris Conley demanded sexual favours in return for a job. Early in 1950, Neilson became pregnant and had her first backstreet abortion.

On November 8 1950, aged 24, she married 41-year-old divorced dentist and Court Club regular George Ellis. He was a violent jealous alcoholic. She left him several times but usually came back. In 1951, while four months pregnant, she appeared in a Diana Dors film Lady Godiva Rides Again. A co-starlet was Joan Collins — neither young actress got a credit.

When daughter Georgina was born, George denied paternity and they separated.

By 1953, Ellis was managing a nightclub popular with racing drivers. She met Blakely, three years her junior, through racing driver Mike Hawthorn. Blakely seemed a well-mannered, posh ex-public schoolboy. He was, in fact, a hard-drinking spoilt brat. Within weeks he moved into Ellis's flat above the club. Ellis became pregnant for the fourth time. Again a backstreet abortion solved the problem.

She started to sleep with rich businessman and ex-RAF pilot Desmond Cussens. When Ellis was sacked as manager of the club, she moved in with Cussens. The relationship with Blakely also continued and became increasingly violent and embittered as Ellis and Blakely both continued liaisons with other people. Blakely proposed marriage and she agreed, but another pregnancy ended with a miscarriage when an angry Blakely punched her in the stomach.

In different ways their two lives both ended on the pavement outside the Magdala on Easter Sunday 60 years ago.

THEY PLAYED THEIR PART IN THE DEFEAT OF FASCISM

WOMEN WHO HELPED WIN THE WAR

Published May 8 2015.

War artists

We owe a special debt of gratitude to Dame Laura Knight. One of the very few female official war artists, she recorded many of the female war heroes. In September 1939 Knight was asked to produce a recruitment poster for the Women's Land Army. Her A Balloon Site, Coventry shows a team of women hoisting a barrage balloon into position.

Her most famous war painting is Ruby Loftus Screwing a Breech Ring. It became the British equivalent of Rosie the Riveter. Knight went to Germany in January 1946 and spent three months observing the Nuremberg trials from inside the courtroom. The result was one of her most moving works, The Nuremberg Trial.

They flew Spitfires

One-hundred-and-sixty-eight women piloted all kinds of fighters and bombers as part of the Air Transport Auxiliary (ATA), which flew over 300,000 flights. These women flew virtually every type flown by the RAF and the Fleet Air Arm, including the four-engined heavy bombers. They delivered aircraft all over the world. Fifteen pilots lost their lives in the air, including aviation pioneer Amy Johnson.

These women pilots received the same pay as men of equal rank. This was the first time that the British government gave equal pay for equal work within any organisation under its control.

D-Day gliders

The very first troops who landed at Pegasus Bridge in the early hours of D-Day were delivered there by Horsa gliders. These cheap and light unpowered aircraft had been towed by bombers from England. The plywood and timber gliders were built by mainly female labour in the Co-op furniture factories of Manchester. Many other aircraft and other armaments were manufactured by huge female workforces who had at last been able to take on skilled engineering jobs.

Bravest of the brave

The war has no greater heroes than the young women agents of the Special Operations Executive (SOE) who were dropped behind enemy lines to liaise with local, often communist, resistance forces in places like occupied France and Yugoslavia. Of SOE's 55 female agents, 13 were killed in action or died in nazi concentration camps.

SOE was also far ahead of contemporary attitudes in its use of women in armed and unarmed combat — those sent into the field were trained to use weapons. We should never forget the bravery of women like Odette Hallowes or Violette Szabo and so many others.

They also served

On, or just behind, the front line were women members of the Auxiliary Territorial Service (ATS). From today's media you would think the only member was a young Princess Elizabeth, but in fact the ATS had 200,000 members.

Bar actually firing guns ATS women did everything a male soldier did. Among them were lorry drivers, motorbike messengers and vehicle maintenance engineers. Women doing the same jobs got the same pay as men. Thousands of female nurses also served in field hospitals and medical posts, often at the front line.

Breaking German codes

The story of Bletchley Park and the breaking of the Enigma codes has got a lot of coverage. Much approbation has gone to Alan Turing and to Tommy Flowers, and those two geniuses certainly deserve much of the credit. But it would be wrong to forget Joan Clarke. Clarke was a leading cryptanalyst and numismatist at Bletchley. Hundreds of other skilled and intelligent women did much of the translation, transcription and complicated calculations involved in unravelling millions of encrypted secret messages.

Not-so-idle women

The badges they wore had the initials IW. Male detractors said it stood for Idle Women, but the women themselves took the insult as a compliment and adopted the name for themselves. In fact IW stood for Inland Waterways and these women kept open one of Britain's most important industrial arteries, the English canal system. The women navigated heavily loaded narrow boats between the London docks and the industrial midlands. Despite bombing raids in the docks and cramped, dirty and uncomfortable conditions on the boats they kept this vital lifeline open.

On the home front

Stella Isaacs founded the Women's Voluntary Service (WVS). Before the war she was in voluntary social work helping the millions of unemployed. When war broke out she was asked to establish an organisation that would assist on the home front. It became the Women's Voluntary Service for Air Raid Precautions Services, later shortened.

The WVS trained millions of women to cope with all kinds of wartime emergencies. They fed, clothed and re-housed enemy air raid victims and organised the evacuation of young children. Issacs was the first woman ever to take up a seat in the House of Lords.

Defending our skies

Women were instrumental in maintaining Britain's massive anti-aircraft defences against the Luftwaffe. Women made and flew huge and ungainly barrage balloons, which held aloft steel cable barriers that forced German bombers to fly above 5,000 feet, thus making bomb aiming much less accurate. More women controlled powerful spotlights that picked out the bombers so that the gun crews could shoot them down. Women worked as spotters and plotters tracking the locations of enemy aircraft for both guns and fighter pursuit.

Helping to feed the nation

The government knew that war would bring food shortages. Britain, then as now, relied heavily on imported food, and German blockades could starve the nation. They encouraged women to work the land. By 1943, more than 80,000 women were part of the Land Army. They did a wide range of jobs, including milking cows, lambing, managing poultry, ploughing, gathering crops, digging ditches and even catching rats. All of these women worked long hours and there was minimal training. They lived either on the farms where they worked, or in hostels. They came from a wide variety of backgrounds, with more than one third from London and other large cities. Their wage was supposed to be £2.85 a week. but many were short changed by greedy farmers.

Lumber Jills

Around 6,000 young women joined the Women's Timber Corps and learned to use saws, axes and heavy lifting tackle to harvest wood needed for the war effort. These women produced the chestnut tracks that allowed troops and tanks to cross soft ground during the D-Day landings, telegraph poles, pit-props, ship masts and the beech plywood that was used to construct Mosquito aircraft and huge D-Day gliders.

SO LONG – IT'S BEEN GOOD TO KNOW YUH

RONNIE GILBERT

Obituary published June 9 2015.

Ronnie Gilbert, folk singer, political activist and the female voice of one of the seminal groups of the post–war US folk revival, the Weavers, has died in San Francisco aged 88.

Born in New York to Jewish immigrant stock, her first diverse musical influences were from her parents. Aged just 10 mum took her to Communist Party rallies where she heard Paul Robeson sing Joe Hill and other labour movement anthems. "It taught me songs are dangerous, songs are subversive and can change your life," she would remember later.

"Dad had different tastes, he loved what he described as Jewish musicals. He taught me his favourite song, Yes, We Have No Bananas. I learned about having fun with music." Gilbert, along with Pete Seeger, Lee Hays and Fred Hellerman, formed the Weavers and the group helped spark a national folk revival with hit recordings of Woody Guthrie's So Long, It's Been Good to Know Yuh and Pete Seeger and Lee Hay's If I Had a Hammer. Their version of Leadbelly's Goodnight Irene was number one in the charts for 13 weeks.

The Weavers sang on picket lines, at union rallies and left-wing fundraisers before becoming enormously popular with wider audiences disenchanted with a US that seemed to be trading WWII for a new cold war. "We sang songs of hope in that strange time after WWII, when already the world was preparing for cold war," Gilbert said in a 1982 interview.

"We still had the feeling that if we could sing loud enough and strong enough and hopefully enough, it would make a difference." Make a huge difference they did. The four, with Gilbert's sweet and strong contralto singing out, launched a vast protest song movement that helped spawn performers like Bob Dylan, Joan Baez, the King-ston Trio and Peter, Paul and Mary and a hundred more who are sing-ing still.

Despite growing popularity among audiences, the anti-communist witch-hunts came thick and fast. The group's success had to battle against the inevitable blacklisting by record companies and TV, radio and music venues. The pressure was relentless. A Weavers' planned television show was cancelled, the group were placed under FBI sur-veillance and Seeger and Hays were called to testify before the House Un-American Activities Committee.

In 1951 the Weavers lost their recording contract with Decca, and by 1953, unable to book most concert venues and banned from ap-pearing on television and radio, they disbanded. They came together again in December 1955 and filled every seat in a concert at Carnegie Hall. Not only was the concert a huge success but independent record label Vanguard released a live album of the event and signed the group for further recordings.

Despite a popular nationwide concert tour, the red-baiting carried on. On January 2 1962, they were told by NBC that their appearance on the Jack Paar TV Show would be cancelled unless they signed a statement disavowing the Communist Party. Gilbert and the other Weavers refused to sign.

The group disbanded in 1964, but Gilbert and the other three Weav-ers occasionally played and sang together during the next 16 years. In 1980, a dying Lee Hays approached the others for one last get-togeth-er. An informal picnic led to a return to Carnegie Hall on November 28 1980. It would the Weavers' last ever major performance except for a benefit for Pete Seeger's Hudson River Clearwater campaign.

Hays would be dead in just a few months, but fortunately the Carn-egie Hall concert and the build-up to it became the documentary The Weavers: Wasn't That a Time!

Gilbert, however, didn't stop singing or protesting. She went on to work variously as a stage actor, a solo singer and then a psychologist and therapist. Various younger singers have recorded and performed with her. She made three albums with Holly Near. She, Seeger and Arlo Guthrie have made an album together.

Her self-authored one-woman show about US labour organiser Mary Harris "Mother" Jones played to packed houses. Gilbert continued to tour and appear in plays, folk festivals and Jewish music festivals well into her eighties.

She also continued her political life, supporting groups such as Women in Black, opposing the Israeli occupation of Palestinian territories.

In 2006, Gilbert and Hellerman accepted a Lifetime Achievement Award at the Grammys on behalf of all the Weavers.

On hearing the sad news about Gilbert I guess there will be a lot of us tonight who listen to, and join in with, a few old and familiar Weavers tracks. "So long Ronnie, it really was good to know yuh."

SHE DEMANDED BREAD AND ROSES

ELIZABETH GURLEY FLYNN

*Published July 1 2015 the 110th anniversary of the founding of
the International Workers of the World. Flynn was one of three
giant Labour movement heroes featured.*

Elizabeth Gurley Flynn was born in 1890 in Concord, New
Hampshire. By the age of 15 she made a public speech on
women under socialism. She began making speeches for the
IWW and that activity got her expelled from school. She was soon
a full-time organiser for the Wobblies. Flynn fought for free speech
for IWW speakers and helped at strikes, including the huge Bread and
Roses strike in Lawrence, Massachusetts, and another at Paterson, New
Jersey.

When WWI started, Elizabeth Gurley Flynn and other IWW leaders opposed the war. Flynn, like many other war opponents at that
time, was charged with espionage. Charges against her were eventually dropped. Flynn defended immigrants like anarchist Emma Goldman, who were being threatened with deportation for opposing the
war. In 1920, Flynn helped found the American Civil Liberties Union
(ACLU). She was active in raising support and money for Italian-born
anarchists Nicola Sacco and Bartolomeo Vanzetti, who were executed
after a shoddy trial found them guilty of murdering two men during
an armed robbery, and she was a key figure in trying to free labour
organisers Thomas J Mooney and Warren K Billings.

For many years ill health restricted Flynn's activism but in 1936 she
joined the Communist Party USA. In 1941, Flynn was elected to the
CPUSA central committee, and the next year she ran for Congress,
stressing women's issues.

After the war ended, as anti-communist sentiment grew Flynn
again found herself defending free speech rights for radicals. In 1951

she and other communists were arrested for conspiracy to overthrow the US government, under the Smith Act of 1940. She was convicted and served a prison term from January 1955 to May 1957.

In 1961 she was elected CPUSA chair, making her the first woman to head that organisation. She remained chair until her death during a trip to Moscow in 1964. She was given a state funeral in Red Square.

Bill Haywood

Big Bill Haywood was one of the most important and colourful leaders of the US and international working class. He led important labour battles from the 1890s until the 1920s.

Born in 1869 in Mormon Salt Lake City, Utah, by the age of nine he was working in the mines to help support his family. He helped organise the militant Western Federation of Miners (WFM), eventually becoming its general secretary. In dozens of strikes Big Bill and the WFN battled court injunctions, state militia, private armies, government intervention, imprisonment, deportation and even lynchings.

The WFM was one of the major forces in founding the Industrial Workers of the World in 1905, just as the workers of Russia were engaged in their first revolution. The IWW's long-range goal was a general strike of the whole working class that would lead to the takeover of industry and the economy.

In 1906 Big Bill was accused of killing the former governor of Idaho. The trial was a government frame-up, engineered by the well-known anti-union Pinkerton detective agency. While in prison, Haywood ran for governor of Idaho. He was acquitted of all charges.

In 1910 he went to Europe, where he helped to organise strikes in Ireland and South Wales. At a conference of the Second International he met Lenin and Rosa Luxemburg and other revolutionaries.

He led the IWW's Lawrence, Massachusetts, 1912 strike of textile workers — the famous Bread and Roses strike. These strikers, mostly recent immigrants and nearly all women, underlined two key target groups of the IWW strategy.

During WWI, the US government launched a witch-hunt against left-wing unions and radical organisations. Big Bill and the IWW were prime targets. He was once again on trial. In 1918 he was found guilty and faced 20 years in jail and a huge fine. He jumped bail and headed for Moscow to join the Communist International Trade Union Bureau. Just before he left he helped found the US Communist Party.

He died in Moscow in 1928 but the name of Big Bill Haywood is still remembered whenever working people fight to defend their rights.

Joe Hill

Joe Hill from Sweden was the greatest song-smith of the Wobblies. We have a special reason for remembering Joe this year because it was 100 years ago, in November 1915, that he was executed on a fitted-up murder charge by the copper mine bosses in Utah.

He learned English during the early 1900s, while working various jobs from New York to San Francisco. As an immigrant worker he frequently faced unemployment. He became a popular songwriter as well as a cartoonist for radical publications.

His most famous songs include The Preacher and the Slave' The Tramp, There is Power in a Union, The Rebel Girl, written as a tribute to Elizabeth Gurney Flynn, and Casey Jones — the Union Scab.

In 1914 two men shot dead John G Morrison, a Salt Lake City area grocer and former policeman, and his son. Hill was convicted of the murders in a controversial trial. Following an unsuccessful appeal, political debates and international calls for clemency from high-profile figures and workers' organisations, Hill was executed.

His famous last words, "Don't mourn, organise" were immortalised in a number of songs. His life and death have inspired songs, books and poems.

Joe Hill was part of what was always an important IWW tactic, the use of song. In the famous Bread and Roses strike in Lawrence the mainly female and mainly immigrant strikers spoke over 50 languages. They could all understand and join in with the labour anthems they found in the IWW publication the Little Red Songbook. The Lawrence action became known as the singing strike.

In the 1960s, the US folk music revival brought a renewed interest in the songs of Joe Hill and other Wobblies. Pete Seeger and Woody Guthrie sang many Wobblie songs from the Little Red Songbook.

However there is no doubt that the song that still has the power to inspire workers more than any other is I Dreamed I Saw Joe Hill Last Night.

SOCIALIST TEDDY FOUGHT UN-BEAR-ABLE CONDITIONS

SYLVIA PANKHURST

Published July 4 2015 as part of the celebration of the Matchwomen's Festival in east London.

A hundred years ago, in 1915, a product was launched in a co-operative women's factory in east London. Let me introduce you to the socialist teddy bear. Our story starts in 1913 as war clouds are gathering. Many of the more right-wing suffragettes are beginning to plan the suspension of their votes for women campaigning and throw their weight behind the jingoistic move towards winning the war.

Sylvia Pankhurst, a socialist suffragette, decides she will spend more of her time and efforts working for the Independent Labour Party in east London. As well as political campaigning — including the battle for equal adult suffrage — Sylvia builds a network of various projects to actually improve the lot of East End women and their families.

She opened mother and baby clinics staffed by doctors who treated patients without charge. She established a milk distribution centre for babies, many of whom were too ill to digest their food. The clinics also distributed Virol malt, eggs and barley, as well as infant health leaflets and feeding charts.

Wartime food shortages and, panic-buying caused food prices to rise rapidly. This began to hit working-class areas like the East End hard. Sylvia's response was to open a cost-price restaurant.

It aimed to serve two-penny, two-course meals to adults and penny meals to children, at midday. Each evening a pint of hot soup and a chunk of bread was available for a penny. Food could be eaten at the restaurant or taken home.

The first restaurant was built by volunteers. Local builders, tradesmen and their families not only gave their labour but also china, cutlery and money. In 1915 they served about 400 meals daily and every day Sylvia was there helping to cook and serve the meals.

Also in 1915 Sylvia realised that children's toys were no longer being imported from Germany. Pre-war Germany had been the toy shop of Europe. Sylvia reckoned a new co-operative toy factory staffed by women would both fulfil the demand for toys and also provide work for many local women who had been thrown on the scrapheap by the closure of many East End sweatshops.

Sylvia's new toy factory employed nearly 60 women and paid them a decent wage compared with the pittance many other local workshops paid. Workers were paid a generous minimum wage of 5d an hour or £1 a week. Conditions were also much better in Sylvia's factory.

The workers turned out a whole range of products. There were wooden toys of all sorts, but no guns, warships or other such hateful products. The wood came from another socialist, George Lansbury, who owned a yard in Bow.

Many of the workers were skilled needlewomen. They designed and made dolls of all colours. They made a whole range of soft stuffed animals. Last but not least, they made the first ever socialist teddy bears.

German toymaker Richard Steiff had introduced a stuffed toy bear in 1903 and it had taken the world by storm. The German Steiff company had dominated the teddy bear market — they still do — but in wartime Britain German bears were both unpatriotic and unobtainable. Sylvia and her co-op stepped in to fill the demand. The socialist bear was born.

To market the bear, Sylvia turned to Gordon Selfridge and his famous Oxford Street store. Selfridge was generally supportive of the suffrage cause. He was a main sponsor of the Suffrage Annual and Women's Who's Who, published in 1913. Selfridge's advertised on the cover and along the foot of every page. Selfridge's also dressed its store windows in the purple, white and green — the colours of the suffragettes.

Sylvia's east London toy factory at was at 45 Norman Road (now Norman Grove), just over a mile from today's Morning Star offices in Bow.

Amy K Browning, who would become a well-known artist, and Hilda Jeffries designed and helped to produce the toys. Edith Downing, a talented sculptor who had trained at the Slade and later been force-fed in prison, modelled sets of realistic wax dolls' heads for the works. Arts and crafts socialist Walter Crane designed some of the toys. Indeed the tradition of the arts and crafts movement, rather than a slavish imitation of German toys, was the work's underlying philosophy.

The range of toys was huge. As well as socialist bears they included pigs, robins and other birds, ducks and ducklings, various dogs, squirrels, and even elephants. Dolls included baby girls and boys, fairies and lifelike wax-headed dolls. The workshop also made dolls' house Chippendale furniture.

Unlike many other suffrage societies, the East London Federation of the Suffragettes (ELFS) did not suspend its suffrage campaigning activities during WWI. The federation was opposed to the war and openly campaigned against conscription, executions for cowardice and wartime restrictions censorship.

Alongside this campaigning Sylvia and ELFS members built an impressive local support network, clinics, nurseries, and restaurants all centred on their Women's Hall on Old Ford Road, and also other centres.

A disused pub, the Gunmakers Arms on Old Ford Road, was refurbished and in April 1915 reopened as a mother and baby clinic, free milk depot and day nursery. Sylvia beautifully renamed it the Mother's Arms.

Sylvia Pankhurst will be remembered for many things; as a militant suffragette, a writer and painter, a socialist and a founder member of the British communist movement. She was a brilliant organiser, a powerful orator and a talented artist and painter. Her paintings of working women are still among the best and most powerful of their kind.

As a journalist she founded and edited two of the best titles in the history of left-wing publications. First the Women's Dreadnought and then the Workers' Dreadnought. She founded the Workers' Socialist Federation in solidarity with the 1917 Russian revolution.

She was a great woman and a great revolutionary, but a fun-loving warm human being too. So I'll finish by paraphrasing my favourite suffragette and socialist slogan from the US: "Give us bread, but give us teddy bears."

LEGENDARY CIVIL RIGHTS ACTIVIST

AMELIA BOYNTON ROBINSON

Obituary published August 28 2015.

In spring this year, on the 50th anniversary of the Bloody Sunday events in Selma, Alabama, Barrack Obama — first black president of the United States — pushed a 103 year old woman in a wheelchair at the head of the commemorative march.

She was Amelia Boynton Robinson, civil rights activist and one of the leaders of the 1965 Selma March. She died in Selma, Alabama, this week aged 104. She had continued to struggle for progressive causes right up until her death.

Amelia Boynton Robinson is perhaps best remembered for the image of her after state troopers attacked the Selma civil rights march with tear gas and batons. The picture of her, unconscious and bloody, flashed around the world and raised sympathy and anger in equal measure wherever it was seen.

On March 7 1965, 600 civil rights marchers headed east out of Selma on US Highway 80. The protest went according to plan until the marchers crossed the Edmund Pettus Bridge and entered Dallas County, where they encountered a wall of state troopers and a huge county posse waiting for them on the other side.

The local sheriff had issued an order for all white males over the age of 21 to report to the courthouse that morning to be deputised.

At the bridge the troopers began shoving the demonstrators, knocking many to the ground and beating them with truncheons. Another detachment of troopers fired tear gas, and mounted troopers charged the crowd on horseback. TV and press images of the brutal attack — with marchers left bloodied and severely injured — won sympathy and support for the Selma voting rights campaigners.

Amelia Boynton, who had helped organise the march as well as marching in it, was beaten unconscious. Photographs of her lying on the road appeared on the front page of newspapers around the world. In fact she was just one of 17 marchers who were hospitalised and another 50 were treated for lesser injuries. The day soon became known as Bloody Sunday.

Selma is a major town in Dallas County, part of the "Alabama black belt" with a majority black population, 80 per cent of whom lived below the poverty line. In 1961 of the 15,000 blacks old enough to vote only 130 were registered. Literacy tests administered unfairly by white registrars kept even educated blacks from registering or voting.

Amelia's husband Sam and son Bruce joined with others to establish the Dallas County Voters League (DCVL) that tried to register black citizens during the late 1950s and early 1960s. Their efforts were blocked by state and local officials, the White Citizens' Council and the Ku Klux Klan. County officials and the Citizens' Council used such tactics as restricted registration hours to stop blacks registering.

The white community also applied economic pressure, including threatening black people's jobs, sacking or evicting them and boycotts of black-owned businesses. There was also much open violence against blacks who tried to register.

In early 1963, Student Nonviolent Co-ordinating Committee organisers Bernard and Colia Liddel Lafayette came Selma to help Amelia's local DCVL. In mid-June, Bernard was beaten and almost killed by klansmen.

When 32 black schoolteachers applied at the county courthouse to register as voters, they were immediately fired by the all-white school board.

Then on July 2 1964, president Lyndon Johnson signed the Civil Rights Act of 1964 into law, prohibiting segregation of public facilities. The act was ignored in Selma and much of the South with Jim Crow laws and customs remaining in effect. Blacks who tried to attend the cinema and eat at the hamburger stand were still beaten and arrested.

On July 6 1964, one of the only two voter registration days that month, 50 black citizens marched to the courthouse to register. The county sheriff arrested them all rather than allow them to apply to vote.

Three days later Judge James Hare issued an injunction that made it illegal for more than two people at a time to talk about civil rights or voter registration in Selma.

It was against this background that Amelia Boynton worked with Dr Martin Luther King, Rosa Parks, James Bevel and many other legendary civil rights heroes. A series of marches were planned between Montgomery and Selma.

One of 10 children, Amelia Platts was born in Savannah, Georgia, on August 18 1911. As a child, she travelled with her mother by horse and buggy to campaign for votes for women. At 14, Amelia entered a college for coloured youth and earned a degree in home economics. She took a job in Dallas County, Alabama, giving instruction in food, nutrition and homemaking in rural households for the department of agriculture.

With her husband, Samuel William Boynton, she spent decades attempting to register black voters. She had managed to register herself in the early '30s. Sam Boynton died in 1963 and the following year Amelia ran for Congress. She was the first woman, black or white, ever to do so. She received about 10 per cent of the vote — a great result given how few blacks had the vote.

In 1990 she was awarded is the Martin Luther King Jr Freedom Medal.

Speaking of her heroic part in the historic Selma civil rights marches she said: "I wasn't looking for notoriety, but if that's what it took I didn't care how many licks I got. It just made me even more determined to fight for our cause."

MOTHER OF THE NOTTING HILL CARNIVAL

CLAUDIA JONES

Published September 1 2015 after the latest Notting Hill Carnival.

Today as it clears up from the biggest carnival in the world, posh Notting Hill — often touted as London's glitterati village — is very different from how it was in the late 1950s. In those days slum landlords like Peter Rachman were letting small rooms at exorbitant rents to mainly West Indian tenants. Those tenants had often been driven into this substandard housing by the racist "No dogs, no blacks" notices in so many other rooms to rent.

Living in Notting Hill in 1959 was a 32-year-old Antiguan immigrant to Britain, a law student, Kelso Cochrane. Walking home one night, Kelso was set upon by a group of racist white youths, who stabbed him with a knife. When three other men arrived on the scene the attackers ran off. Cochrane died an hour later in hospital. Some 1,200 people joined his funeral procession to Kensal Green Cemetery. The police declared that this was not a racist murder — where have we heard that before?

It was standard police procedure to deny any racial motive to crimes of this sort. It often still is. Police thinking at the time was that to arrest a white man for a black murder would cause enormous civil unrest.

In fact at the time Notting Hill was a stronghold for Oswald Mosley's fascist Union Movement and Colin Jordan's just as nasty White Defence League. The previous year, race riots had broken out in the area. We now know that Cochrane's killers were teddy boy supporters of Mosley and his fascists. Peter Dawson, a member himself, said as much to the Sunday People.

Mosley later held a public meeting on the exact spot where Cochrane had been murdered. He stood here in the 1959 general election on a stridently anti-immigration platform. Mosley demanded forced repatriation of Caribbean immigrants as well no mixed marriages.

As a reaction to Cochrane's murder and the Notting Hill race riots, in 1959, local communist activist and journalist Claudia Jones organised events to celebrate Caribbean culture in what she called "the face of the hate from the white racists."

These events laid the foundations for what would become the first Notting Hill Carnival in 1964. It would grow and grow until today it is one of the biggest street festivals in the world attracting over a million people.

Jones was born a Cumberbatch — her family slave name. Actor Benedict Cumberbatch's ancestors made their fortune from slavery and gave their slaves the family name. Today Benedict is horrified by his family's disgusting history.

Born in 1915, Claudia would have been 100 this year. Trinidad-born, as a child she migrated with her family to the US.

In 1936 she joined the Young Communist League USA. By 1937 she was writing for the US Daily Worker. Just one year later she was editor of its Weekly Review. The Young Communist League renamed itself American Youth for Democracy during World War II, Jones became editor of its monthly journal, Spotlight.

After the war, she held leading roles in the Women's National Commission, the Communist Party USA women's commission, and the National Peace Council. She also made a major contribution to the US civil rights movement.

However her membership of the national committee of the Communist Party and her various activities led in 1948 to her arrest and imprisonment. It was to be the first of four terms in jail. These periods would break her health but never her spirit.

All her effective communist writing and campaigning was too much for the FBI and the rest of the US red-baiting witch-hunt machine. The US authorities had at first wanted to deport her to Trinidad and Tobago. Governor Major General Sir Hubert Elvin Rance considered that "she may prove troublesome" and refused to take her.

She was eventually offered residency in Britain on humanitarian grounds. Jones arrived in Britain in 1955. By 1958 she had founded Britain's first black newspaper, the West Indian Gazette and Afro-Asian Caribbean News. From its office above a barber's shop in Brixton she used the paper to campaign against racism in housing, education and employment.

Through her paper she became a key figure in the rise of consciousness within the black British community. All the while she spoke at peace rallies and the Trades Union Congress, against immigration legislation and for Nelson Mandela's release. She visited Russia and China, where she met Mao Zedong.

Just four months after launching her paper, race riots hit the streets of Notting Hill and some other British cities including Nottingham. Jones met many of the members of the black British community to discuss these worrying developments.

She also had talks with black colonial leaders such as Cheddi Jagan of Guiana, Norman Manley of Jamaica and Eric Williams of Trinidad and Tobago.

Jones decided the black community needed to "wash the taste of Notting Hill and Nottingham out of our mouths." She used her connections to book St Pancras Town Hall in January 1959 for the first Mardi-Gras-based carnival. Jazz guitarist Fitzroy Coleman and singer Cleo Laine were among the headline acts. This and five other London events raised money "to assist the payments of fines of coloured and white youths involved in the Notting Hill events." It was those early carnival events that would grow into the huge carnival we know today.

Claudia Jones died on Christmas Eve 1964. She was buried near Karl Marx in Highgate Cemetery.

A message from her lifelong friend and comrade Paul Robeson told the many assembled mourners: "It was a great privilege to have known Claudia Jones. She was a vigorous and courageous leader of the Communist Party of the United States, and was very active in the work for the unity of white and coloured peoples and for dignity and equality, especially for the negro people and for women."

In 2008, Britain's Royal Mail issued a Claudia Jones postage stamp. In the same year, a blue plaque was unveiled on the corner of Tavistock Road and Portobello Road commemorating Jones as the "Mother of Caribbean Carnival in Britain."

NOT JUST JAM AND JERUSALEM
THE WOMEN'S INSTITUTE

Published September 7 2015 the centenary of the campaigning and much-maligned women's organisation.

O K, let's get the jokes over with. Everyone knows the Women's Institute is just about making jam, wearing big hats and posing for nude calendars. Oh yes, and singing Jerusalem.

Well, I'll own up: I just love William Blake and Hubert Parry's amazing anthem. I've sung it at communist comrades' funerals, on protest marches, hiking to the site of the Kinder Trespass and (whisper it quietly) I've even sung it at a meeting of my local WI.

My talk to the WI was on the Kinder Trespass and the battle for access to the countryside. The WI members' attitude was spot on, heartwarming and encouraging. My speaker's fee was a delicious date and walnut loaf baked by one of the members.

We sang Jerusalem, and then Ewan McColl's Manchester Rambler — the song McColl wrote for the Trespass. They knew all the words. We finished the musical spot with some amazing jazz piano improvisations from a 93-year-old member.

My evening with them completely changed my mind about the WI, although to tell the truth I've always been a regular customer for their mulberry jam on sale at the WI stall at our local market.

Even this dyed-in-the-wool atheist has some sympathy with the handwritten label on the jar. It says in neat italic script: "God could undoubtedly have made a better tasting berry but God undoubtedly didn't."

The first Women's Institute was formed in 1897 in Stoney Creek, Ontario, Canada. And then as WWI got underway in 1915 Britain got its first WI.

The very first branch was in Anglesey, Wales. The village was Llanfairpwllgwyngyllgogerychwyrndrobwllllantysiliogogogoch — you couldn't make it up. I bet the needlewomen who sewed that very first WI banner wished they lived in Ely.

Many of the early leaders and members were active in the women's suffrage movement. They understood the need to encourage the fuller participation of women in public life.

Three years later, in 1918, there were nearly 200 WI branches. Their first resolution urged local authorities to take advantage of the government scheme for state-aided housing.

In 1920 they won one of their first great victories for women. They campaigned for the Bastardy Bill that sought to make unmarried fathers responsible for the upkeep of their illegitimate children. At the same time the WI urged its members to stand for parish and district councils. By 1920 the WI had its first MP. Margaret Winteringham was secretary of the WI in Lindsey, Lincolnshire. She was only the third female MP in Britain.

In 1922 the WI urged more public health education to prevent venereal disease — an amazingly bold move at such an early date.

In 1924 they adopted Jerusalem as their anthem. They have been singing it ever since.

The year 1933 saw the call for all WI members to support local efforts to deal with mass unemployment and distress it caused.

Other political campaigns sought to improve water supplies in villages, for the preservation of ancient buildings and for better medical care of pregnant women in rural areas.

In 1938 as war clouds gathered the WI made early plans for wartime evacuation of children. Later a WI report became a major part of the argument that lead to the 1945 Labour government setting up family allowances.

During WWII Lady Denman, head of the WI, was asked to head a re-formed Women's Land Army. The Ministry of Food allocated sugar to WI preservation centres in order to make jam. Members gathered wild rose hips to make vitamin C-rich syrup to replace almost unobtainable imported orange juice.

Some better-off WI members donated their unwanted fur coats to Clementine Churchill's Aid to Russia fur scheme. "Give your Sable to Uncle Joe Stalin" was the slogan.

As early as 1939 the WI was demanding that, when peace came, equal facilities for full education at all levels should be provided in town and country and that men and women should receive equal pay for equal work.

In 1947 WI campaigns won the right for rural midwives to use pain-relieving analgesics and the right for parents to visit their sick children in hospital.

In 1954 the institute started a national anti-litter campaign. It would lead to the Keep Britain Tidy Group. By 1956 members were protesting against the withdrawal of country bus and rail services.

As early as 1960 the WI was voicing concern about the use of toxic sprays and urging more stringent controls on chemicals such as DDT. In 1961 it pledged to support the Freedom from Hunger campaign.

In 1962 the WI expressed concern about the dangers of nuclear radiation, joining with other women's organisations to demand a reduction in nuclear testing.

In 1972 it called for a full free family planning service and for more nursery education.

Just one year later it demanded a national policy for recycling and reducing waste. It was well ahead of its times with such radical policies.

For its diamond jubilee it nailed its colours firmly to the mast. The WI said it "believes in the principle of equality of opportunity and of legal status for men and women and pledges itself to work to achieve this."

In the early 1980s the all-women peace camp at Greenham Common changed British politics forever. When some media portrayed the protesters as a witches' coven of hard-left criminals and a threat to family values, protesters declaring their long-standing membership of the WI painted a very different picture.

The 1986 AGM pushed for more public information about Aids. In 1993 the WI became founding members of the Fair Trade Foundation.

In 2000 they famously gave Tony Blair the clap — a slow handclap, that is — when he tried to turn his speech at its AGM into a party-political broadcast. By 2001 it was campaigning again, this time to save rural post offices.

All this year the WI is holding various centenary celebrations although one — a royal garden party — turned sour when the initial invitation list had to be pared down by 500 members who had already paid for their tickets and mostly bought, or perhaps made, new outfits and hats. The unlucky members were told they could no longer attend the party.

A hasty face-saving exercise by the palace had the Duchess of Cambridge showing interest in her local WI. So far Kate has neither joined in with Jerusalem or made a pot of jam. I think perhaps the WI will do just as well without her as it enters its next 100 years of campaigns.

UNSUNG HEROES OF THE BATTLE OF BRITAIN
WOMEN FLYERS

Published on Battle of Britain Day September 15 2015.

As Britain celebrates the 75th anniversary of the Battle of Britain, you might be led to believe that the war was won by stereotypical Boris Johnson lookalikes flying their Spitfires from pretty aerodromes somewhere on the South Downs.

After a sunny afternoon shooting down the Hun, they would hop into the red MG to spend the evening in the village pub with some sporting gels in pretty frocks or Air Transport Auxiliary uniforms and listening to Churchill or the king on the bakelite wireless set. This stereotype of the Battle of Britain might be comical if it wasn't so tragically wrong.

It is true that during the war there were some brave ex-public school university students going into combat, and dying, within 24 hours of enlisting, but there were also working-class heroes from all over Britain, Europe and the Commonwealth flying Spitfires and Hurricanes — and women flew planes too.

Mohinder Singh Pujji was one of 18 qualified Indian pilots to join the RAF in 1940. A disgraceful official RAF colour bar was only removed in 1939.

After being hit in one aerial dogfight, Pujji's Sikh turban filled with blood. After that he always carried a spare turban, but wearing it in combat meant that he could not wear an oxygen mask and one of his lungs was irreparably damaged at high altitude.

Pujji was just one of the pilots from foreign lands who fought in the skies above England in that long summer of 1940. At least 595, one in five of the 2,936 Battle of Britain fighter pilots, were not British.

They included 145 Poles, 127 New Zealanders, 112 Canadians, 88 Czechoslovaks, 10 Irish, 32 Australians, 28 Belgians, 25 South Africans, 13 French, seven US citizens, three Southern Rhodesians and one each from Jamaica and Palestine.

Among those killed were 47 Canadians and the same number of New Zealanders, 24 Australians, 17 from South Africa, 35 Poles, 20 Czechs and six Belgians. Even this impressive roll of honour may not tell the whole story.

Aubrey de Lisle Inniss, for instance, came from Barbados. During the battle, he flew a Bristol Blenheim night fighter and shot down a nazi bomber. Despite his place of birth, the official RAF roll of honour lists him as British. From wherever they came, Britain or abroad, we owe them all a huge debt of gratitude.

In the battle of Britain, the objective of the nazi Luftwaffe was to achieve air superiority over the RAF's Fighter Command.

They started by bombing coastal shipping convoys and ports such as Portsmouth. A month later the main targets were RAF airfields. Then came raids on factories involved in aircraft production.

The workforces in these factories were mainly female. Heavy raids failed to lower either morale or production. Finally Hitler ordered the heavy bombing of civilian populations in towns and cities.

The Battle of Britain stopped Hitler gaining air superiority. He was forced to postpone and eventually cancel Operation Sea Lion, his plan to invade Britain. It was the nazis' first significant defeat of the war.

After his planned invasion Hitler had hoped for a negotiated peace with Britain. Many British aristocrats and members of the royal family were certainly in sympathy with the nazi cause and ready to do a deal with Hitler. Just a few weeks before Germany invaded Poland, King George VI and his wife, the late Queen Mother, sent Hitler a birthday greeting.

The king and queen and daughters Elizabeth — now queen in her own right — and Margaret have, of course, been seen recently practising their nazi salutes in a 1930s royal home movie. King George's brother, the former King Edward VIII, who became the Duke of Windsor after abdicating in 1936 pronounced: "I never thought Hitler was such a bad chap."

Lord Rothermere, owner of the Daily Mail, was another friend and supporter of Hitler. One Rothermere editorial told Daily Mail readers: "The minor misdeeds of individual nazis would be submerged by the immense benefits the new regime is already bestowing upon Germany."

It has been largely forgotten that women were another equally important band of fliers who played a key role in the victory over the nazis in the skies over Britain. Banned from actual combat, this elite group of aviators helped keep our overstretched fighter squadrons supplied with new and repaired aircraft to replace losses.

Delivering often unfamiliar aircraft in all kinds of weather, often without the aid of radar and radio, the 164 female Air Transport Auxiliary (ATA) pilots suffered heavy losses. Proportionately the female casualty rate was higher than that of male fighter pilots.

During the war these female heroes faced incredible jealously and sexism and it's only now, 75 years later, that their exploits are being properly recognised. The first eight women signed up on New Year's Day 1940. They were initially paid 20 per cent less than the men. Not until 1943 did the women finally achieve equal pay.

Legendary pioneering aviator Amy Johnson was the first female pilot to die in ATA service. Her Airspeed Oxford crashed into the Thames estuary in 1941. A further 15 ATA women pilots would pay the ultimate price. One was Margaret Fairweather, who lost her pilot husband while she was pregnant, but got back into the cockpit soon after her baby was born. She escaped one crash landing only to die in another crash in 1944.

The female pilots faced opposition from jealous male colleagues. Accusations of incompetence and lesbianism were common. There was even sabotage.

Charles G Grey, editor of Aeroplane magazine, had written: "The menace is the woman who thinks that she ought to be flying in a high-speed bomber when she really has not the intelligence to scrub the floor of a hospital properly." It was Grey's keen support for both

Hitler and Mussolini, rather than his sexism, however that cost him his job as editor.

So let us leave the last word on these brave women to Lord Beaverbrook, owner of the Daily Express and Churchill's minister of aircraft production. "They were soldiers fighting in the struggle just as completely as if they had been engaged on the battlefront. Without them the pilots in the Battle of Britain would never have got off the ground."

ANTI-TRADE UNION ACTIONS IN AMBRIDGE

YSANNE CHURCHMAN

Published October 2 2015, 60 years after commercial television first appeared in Britain.

Sixty years ago on September 23 1955 commercial television arrived in Britain. Actually it only arrived in London and a few surrounding areas and only about 100,000 people had sets capable of receiving the new channel.

Even so BBC founder Lord Reith was horrified at the breaking of the corporation's monopoly. He feared it would bring an invasion of US-style programming. "Somebody introduced dog racing into England," he said. "And somebody introduced smallpox, bubonic plague and the black death.

"Somebody is minded now to introduce sponsored broadcasting into this country ... Need we be ashamed of moral values, or of intellectual and ethical objectives? It is these that are here and now at stake."

Reith wanted something done. He ordered his Home Service station controller to send a memo asking The Archers' writers to kill off a major character on the night of ITV's launch. Of course the first director general and his BBC management team denied it had intended to try to smother its new rival at birth.

The Archers' script writers set it up beautifully. On the night before the ITV launch they had Grace Archer, the young, attractive and popular wife of Phil Archer plunge into a blazing barn to rescue her horse Midnight. The last scene, a real cliffhanger, had Grace trapped by a falling beam and her brave husband Phil rushing in to try a rescue.

No wonder the next evening some eight million listeners tuned in to hear the show and the sad news that Grace had died in Phil's arms. The BBC switchboard was jammed with fans in tears. Hundreds of wreaths arrived at Broadcasting House.

The BBC's cover story for Grace Archer's headline-grabbing death was that the show had too many characters and they needed to get rid of one.

In fact, earlier that year the controller of the BBC Light Programme had said in a memo: "The more I think about it, the more I believe that a death of a violent kind in The Archers timed, if possible, to diminish interest in the opening of commercial television in London, is a good idea."

But why was Grace chosen? A recent BBC docudrama has revealed the true story and it is one of crude, but not unexpected anti-trade union activity by the BBC. After all we now know that for many years the corporation had an MI5 office in its headquarters simply to vet employees for left-wing, socialist or simply pro-trade union views. The actress playing the part of Grace was Ysanne Churchman. Unlike many of the Archers cast she was a keen member and supporter of Equity — the actors union.

The man who invented The Archers was Godfrey Baseley and he ran the programme as his own fiefdom. He liked the cast, writers and technicians to call him God. Baseley paid actors as he felt fit, he argued that Churchman didn't need the same wage as male stars as she had a husband with a good salary.

He also liked to use local rustic amateurs in small parts, paying them little or nothing at all. Ysanne demanded equal pay with male stars and threatened to bring in Equity if she didn't get it. She also encouraged her fellow cast members to join the union at a time where the Equity closed shop was far from universal.

The battle between the young actress and Baseley had been long and bitter — the year before he had written her out of the storyline by sending her character to Ireland for many months. That didn't stop her recruiting members for Equity or her demand for equal pay. When the instruction came down from above to kill off a major character he quickly decided that this could solve the problem of his studio floor militant.

Churchman, now aged 90, in a postscript to the drama documentary confirmed she was subjected to victimisation from Baseley. It was "victimisation because I'd been to Equity to get my fees put right," she revealed. She wanted the same pay as her male co-stars, and for actors to be in the union.

WOMEN'S FOOTBALL, THE GAME THE FA COULDN'T KILL

Published December 31 2015 in memory of a disgraceful period in British football 95 years ago.

Come back with me to Boxing Day 1920. We are at Everton's ground, Goodison Park, in Liverpool for the traditional post Christmas match. The ground is full to capacity, 53,000 fans, indeed there are 14,000 more locked outside unable to get in.

But it isn't Everton the crowds have come to see. It is two women's sides, Dick, Kerr Ladies from Preston are playing the ladies of St Helen's, two of the best of the many female teams dominating the sport in the years just after World War I.

The match had been organised to raise money for the Unemployed Ex-Servicemen's Distress Fund in Liverpool. It raised £3,115 (£623,000 in today's money). For comparison, today Everton men's best gate in the 2014-15 season was 39,000.

Florrie Redford, Kerr star striker, missed her train to Liverpool but captain and right back Alice Kell moved up to centre forward and scored a second-half hat-trick, giving the Preston side a 4-0 victory.

Two weeks later the Kerr played a game at Old Trafford, the home of Manchester United, this time to raise money for ex-servicemen in Manchester.

Over 35,000 people watched the game and £1,962 (£392,000) was collected.

Earlier in 1920, the first ever women's international game had taken place. Kerr beat a French XI 2-0 at Herne Hill. 25,000 had watched that match.

As 1921 dawned everything seemed set for the development of women's football as a major sport.

However, the blazered colonel blimps, all men of course, running the Football Association had other ideas. They decided this was the year to ban women's football from all official FA club grounds.

They pompously declared that football was "quite unsuitable for females." It would remain that way until the 1970s. The huge setback their ban caused is still felt in the game today.

Women's football had started in the 1890s and in north London 10,000 fans watched a game at Crouch End between teams representing north and south London. North won 7-1.

The biggest growth in the popularity of women's football came during the first world war when women were called on to do factory jobs left by the men who had gone to fight. As men marched away to the trenches, they were replaced by women.

Millions of women took on jobs that had previously been considered men's work, from precision engineering to working the land.

The number of women employed increased from 3.25 million in 1914 to almost five million in January 1918. Nearly 200,000 women worked in government departments.

Half a million became clerical workers. Women worked as conductors on trams and buses. 250,000 worked on the land.

The greatest increase of female workers was in engineering. Over 700,000 women worked at highly skilled and very dangerous jobs in munitions factories doing all sorts of work that had previously been considered far too difficult for women. Unsurprisingly they did the it just as well, if not better, than any man.

Just like the men before them, the women working in factories began to play football during lunch-breaks. Teams were formed and on Christmas Day in 1916, a game took place between Ulverston Munitions Girls — the Munitionettes — and another group of local women. The Munitionettes won 11-5.

Similar games between rival factories took place in South Wales while in London the Hackney Marshes National Projectile Factory team took on all comers.

The Dick, Kerr factory in Preston produced locomotives, trams, cable drums, pontoon bridges, cartridge boxes and munitions. By 1917 it was producing 30,000 shells per week.

The women at the factory decided they should form a football team. On Christmas Day 1917, they organised a charity match in aid of the local hospital for wounded soldiers. The game took place at Preston North End's ground which had not been used since the FA men's programme was cancelled after the outbreak of the war.

Over 10,000 people turned up to watch the women's game. Kerr beat the Arundel Foundry 4-0. They went on to play and beat other north-west factories.

Soon the fans were cheering on new heroes such as captain Kell, Redford and the hard-tackling defender Lily Jones. When they played and lost to Lancaster Ladies, three of the opposing team, Jennie Harris, Jessie Walmsley and Anne Hastie were persuaded to come and work at the Dick, Kerr factory and play football for them. This poaching would become a regular way of building the team.

Women's football, it seemed, was here to stay. Then at the end of the first world war the men came home. Most women were forced out of their jobs in the munitions factories and elsewhere. However, the interest in football did not die.

Some enlightened employers continued to support women's teams. The Dick, Kerr factory was one of these and its women's team went on from strength to strength. They became Preston Ladies. Sutton Glass Works women's football team reformed as St Helens Ladies' AFC.

And so the scene was set for that Boxing Day match in 1920. Despite the men of the FA's worst intentions, women's football never died.

However, the 1921 FA ban meant that by the 1920s and '30s women's teams found it impossible to find good grounds to play matches.

An attempt to form and sustain a Ladies Football Association ended in failure and the women's game failed to develop any formal structure. The women arranged charity matches but there were never enough teams to hold a proper women's league.

In September 1937, Preston Ladies beat Edinburgh Ladies 5-1 to win the Championship of Great Britain and the World. A World Championship victory dinner was held at Booths Cafe in Preston.

Preston Ladies, the previous Dick, Kerr team, had played 437 matches, won 424, lost seven and drawn six. They scored 2,863 goals and had only 207 scored against them. They had raised over £100,000 for charity.

World War II saw women again doing work that had since the end of WWI been again exclusively for men. Factories, transport, mills, farms, even our canals continued to serve the nation in the safe hands of women.

Preston Ladies played only a few games during the second world war. Petrol rationing made it almost impossible to get to away games. The FA still refused to lift its ban on women's football.

In 1947 the Kent County FA suspended a referee because he was working as a manager and trainer with Kent Ladies Football Club. It justified its decision with the comment that "women's football brings the game into disrepute."

In 1946 Lily Parr was made captain of Preston Ladies in recognition of over a quarter of a century's service. She had only missed five games since joining the team in 1920. She had scored 967 goals out of the team's total of 3,022.

Today, the Morning Star's sports section confirms women's football is alive and well, although it is still sidelined by the male-dominated FA establishment. Despite that it becomes more popular every day — understandable when England's women's team outshines our men in every world competition.

It is time then to remember, and give thanks to, those early female pioneers who kept the flame burg and the ball in the air over the last 95 years of women's football.

A VISION OF AN IRELAND FREE, UNITED AND SOCIALIST

MADGE DAVISON

*Published in February to remember a comrade and
friend who died tragically early*

Back in 1971 I was editor of the Young Communist League magazine Challenge. I was lucky enough to interview Madge Davison a leading young communist activist from Belfast.

Madge was in London to join one of the huge anti-Vietnam war demonstrations. She had already gained a reputation in the anti-war movement when in May 1968 she threw herself in front of marching sailors from a US destroyer as they took part in the Belfast Lord Mayor's parade.

I interviewed her about Northern Ireland for Challenge, many of us characterised the six counties as Britain's Vietnam — a country occupied by a foreign army and fighting for its own independence.

She told the young Challenge readers of the outrages being committed by British soldiers in the streets of her native Belfast, as well as of Derry and of other towns in the North.

The people in Northern Ireland were being forced to build barricades and use petrol bombs to defend working-class areas from armed police and British soldiers harassing the local population with snatch raids and random searches and arrests.

She told us of her part of a several hundred-strong women's march against the Falls Road curfew that had been imposed by the occupying forces of the British army.

She also spoke of her political work with the Northern Ireland Civil Rights Association (NICRA) for which she had become a full-time organiser.

Her insights were to be proved prophetic. Just months later, on January 30 1972, the British army shot 26 unarmed civilians on the streets of Derry. Fourteen people died.

These events became known as Bloody Sunday sometimes called the Bogside Massacre. Many of the victims were shot while fleeing from the soldiers and some were shot while trying to help the wounded. Two protesters were also injured when they were run down by army vehicles.

Madge, as a full-time organiser for NICRA had played a leading role in organising the march. I well remember watching the huge amount of TV news coverage of the events and seeing Madge at the heart of the action. She went on to organise marches and protests about the Bloody Sunday murders and was a key player in getting the impressive memorial to the victims built.

As well as her leading role NICRA, Madge was a member of the national executive committee of the Communist Party of Ireland (CPI) and the first general secretary of its youth wing the Connolly Youth Movement after it became an all-Ireland body in 1970.

Madge Davidson came from a working-class Protestant background in the Shore Road area of Belfast. She was particularly proud of her Presbyterian background, of the great contributions made by her forebears in the Society of the United Irishmen.

This gave her a unique understanding that religious differences were never as important as they could sometimes seem. She worked all her life for the unity of the Protestant and Catholic sections of the working class.

Madge was deeply influenced by another outstanding Belfast communist woman Betty Sinclair. Although 40 years older than Madge, she became a mentor, comrade and friend.

Madge was an outstanding internationalist. She led her Connolly Youth Movement to protest when US communist Angela Davis was framed for murder.

She had the capacity to involve a wide range of young people in progressive action. In 1973 she organised and led a 114-strong all Ireland delegation to the 10th World Festival of Youth and Students in East Berlin.

She involved young people from the Connolly Youth Movement, the Republican Movement, Union of Students in Ireland, Young Liberals, National Federation of Youth Clubs, Irish Union of School Students, NICRA as well as young trade unionists.

She arranged for the delegation to visit the grave of legendary Irish anti-fascist Frank Ryan, commander of the Connolly Column of the International Brigades.

Frank's grave was in Dresden but his body has since been returned to his beloved Dublin where he has an honoured place in the republican section of Glasnevin Cemetery.

When her work with NICRA finally finished Madge went to Queen's University obtaining a first-class honours degree in law. She was called to the bar in 1984 soon establishing a reputation as a human rights and women's rights barrister.

Late in 1990 she won a senior post with the Fair Employment Agency but in January 1991 she was diagnosed with cancer. She died aged just 41 on January 27 1991.

In her all-too-short life she achieved more than many do in twice as many years. Speaking at her funeral Michael O'Riordan, then general secretary of the CPI, said: "Madge was motivated by a vision, a dream of a society in which there would be no sectarianism, no exploitation, one in which men and women would live in equality, one in which poverty would be abolished — in short, an Ireland free, united, and socialist."

That vision is yet to be realised but wherever that fight goes on the memory of Madge Davison will always be an inspiration.

THE WOMEN OF THE EASTER RISING

To be published Easter 2016 to remember the brave Irish women who played a key role in the declaration of the Irish republic 100 years before

As a watery dawn broke on Easter Monday 1916, Winnie Carney entered the General Post Office on O'Connell Street along with her many armed republican comrades, men and women. Most carried arms and ammunition, Winnie carried a heavier load.

Winnie was secretary and assistant to James Connolly, head of the Irish Citizen Army. She did carry her Webley revolver but more importantly she carried a heavy typewriter. Connolly, she knew would need to send clear typed orders all over the city in the battle that was to come.

When Connolly was wounded Winnie refused to leave his side despite direct orders from Padraig Pearse and from Connolly himself. Carney, alongside Elizabeth O'Farrell and Julia Gremen only left the GPO with the rest of the rebels after their surrender.

After her capture, she was held in Kilmainham Gaol and was then moved to Mountjoy Prison. Carney, alongside Helena Molony, Maria Prolz, Brigid Foley and Ellen O'Ryan and others were moved to an English prison at Aylesbury.

Sixty-nine other women were released from prison one week after the execution of the rising's leaders. Women had played their part in every part of Dublin where the fighting took place with just one exception.

At Boland's Mill, Eamon de Valera defied of the orders of Pearse and Connolly to allow women fighters into the garrison. He would confirm his anti-woman prejudice in his many years as president of Ireland.

Early in the day one of the best-known republican women Countess Constance Markievicz shot a Royal Irish Constabulary member in the head near St Stephen's Green. Later the same day, she was sniping at British troops in the city centre.

Countess Constance was born to an aristocratic London family with a home in County Sligo. She rejected society life and turned, first to painting and then to politics. She married a man who claimed he was a Polish Count.

During the great lock-out organised by Jim Larkin in 1913 she had ran a soup kitchen from the Irish Transport and General Workers Union headquarters at Liberty Hall.

James Connolly became a significant influence in the development of Constance's political ideology. She became a commissioned officer in Connolly's Irish Citizen Army. At Easter 1916 she fought in St Stephen's Green and then the College of Surgeons.

She was sentenced to death, commuted to life imprisonment because of her gender. She protested that she just wanted to die with her comrades, who were being executed almost daily in the yard outside her cell in Kilmainham.

Later Constance Markievicz would become the first woman to be elected to the Westminster Parliament but she refused to take her seat. She was also the first woman to be elected to and serve in Dail Eireann. She became the first female minister in any modern democracy, as minister for labour at the first meeting of the Dail in 1919.

Helena Moloney was among the soldiers who attacked the British headquarters at Dublin Castle. British soldiers couldn't understand what made these dozens of women fight and even die for a free Ireland.

Women volunteers like Margaretta Keogh one of those who paid the ultimate sacrifice alongside their many male comrades.

Prior to 1916, many women across Ireland had been involved in various organisations, dedicated to the fight to win equal rights for women.

Many women, and not a few men, believed that when the battle for Irish independence was won women's rights and suffrage might be easier to achieve.

Women joined the struggle in organisations like The Irish Women's Workers Union, Inghinidhe Na hEireann (Daughters of Ireland), The Irish Women's Franchise League and Cumann na mBan (League of Women).

As the fight for a free Irish Republic grew, culminating in the declaration of a republic by Pearse on Easter morning many women inside the garrisons fought alongside the men.

Women had proved to be excellent at gathering vital intelligence out and about. Many others carried dispatches and moved arms from dumps across the city to insurgent strongholds. On the streets of Dublin squads of women marched in their dark green uniforms and slouch hats. Many had revolvers strapped to their sides.

One of the female revolutionaries, Margaret Skinnider, wrote in her book Doing My Bit for Ireland: "Whenever I was called down to carry a dispatch, I took off my uniform, put on my dress and hat, and went out the side door of the college with my message. As soon as I returned, I slipped back into my uniform."

Rose McNamara was in command of the 21-strong female battalion at the Marrowbone Lane Distillery. After surrender the women of the garrison could have evaded arrest but they marched down four-deep in uniform along with the men.

Molony, an actress and journalist who served alongside Dr Kathleen Lynn at City Hall during Easter week and had smuggled guns to Ireland from England for the rising, said: "I had an Irish tweed costume, with a Sam Browne belt. I had my own revolver and ammunition."

When it became clear that the battle for the GPO was lost Pearse selected nurse O'Farrell to officially surrender to the British authorities. She had acted as a dispatch rider before and during the rising delivering orders and instructions to the outposts around Dublin.

She was one of three women, who remained in the GPO until the very end. She and her lifelong friend and fellow nurse Julia Grenan were caring for the wounded including Connolly.

At 12.45pm on Saturday April 29, O'Farrell took a Red Cross insignia and a white flag and emerged into heavy fire on Moore Street beside the GPO to surrender to the British military.

British soldiers dragged her to Brigadier General William Lowe. Lowe sent her back to Pearse with a demand for unconditional surrender. Pearse and O'Farrell finally surrendered to General Lowe. The battle for the GPO was over but the battle for Irish freedom moved up a gear.

O'Farrell's work wasn't over. She dodged sniper fire and British checkpoints while criss-crossing the city convincing local rising leaders that the decision to capitulate was genuine.

Over 100 women took part directly in the rising. More than half were members of the republican organisation Cumann na mBan, committed to the use of force against the British occupation of Ireland as well as fighting for female equality. Both those struggles continue today.

Also available from Manifesto Press:

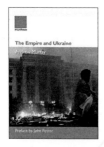

The Empire and Ukraine
Andrew Murray
£11.95 ISBN 978-1-907464-13-3
Murray sets the Ukraine crisis in its global and local context, and draws the lessons needed for the anti-war movement as great power conflict returns to Europe and threatens a new cold war or worse.

Proud Journey: A Spanish Civil War memoir
Bob Cooney
£5 ISBN 978-1-907464-14-0
Published for the first time, International Brigader Bob Cooney's memoir takes us from clashes with the Blackshirts in Aberdeen to the battlefields of Spain.

Global Education 'Reform'
edited by Gawain Little
£7.99 ISBN 978-1-907464-12-6
Brings together contributions by leading educationalists at an international teachers' conference part organised by the National Union of Teachers in 2014. Foreword by NUT general secretary Christine Blower.

for more information (and many more titles) visit www.manifestopress.org.uk